Felix E. Oppenheim

University of Massachusetts

Moral

Principles

in Political

Philosophy

RANDOM HOUSE

New York

Moral Principles

in Political Philosophy

Studies in Political Science

to Sulamite

Preface

"Political Theory," listed by political science departments in catalogues of American colleges and universities, is most likely a label for a course in the history of political thought. Courses in "political philosophy," offered with increasing frequency by philosophy departments, also tend to use the historical approach. On the other hand, courses in economic and psychological theory are more often organized from a systematic point of view; sociological theory courses tend to move in this direction; the same is also true of courses in ethics (or ethical theory). There are good reasons for this difference. The historical dimension is indispensable to an understanding of the close interrelationships between political theories and political systems, political ideologies and political beliefs, political thought and political action. Even so, the comparison with other social and behavioral sciences suggests the possibility that the historical approach to the study of politcal theory could be supplemented (but not superseded) by a more analytic treatment. There is a further argument. Because of the great strides made by analytic philosophy in the last decades, it seems a good time to apply its methods and results to the study of political theory—more specifically, to apply one particular area of analytic philosophy, moral philosophy, to one particular area of political theory, political ethics.

This study endeavors to do just that, concentrating on a single, but crucial, question: Is it possible to demonstrate that certain basic principles of political ethics are objectively true or false, regardless of subjective moral commitments, and if so, by what method? Various answers to this question are illustrated by examples from classical and modern political philosophies. Instead of appearing in chronological order, they have been grouped according to the type of answer they provide. In the selection of authors to be discussed, I have been guided by a single consideration, that they should supply good examples for each of these alternative views. Nonetheless, the majority of the "great" political thinkers usually dealt with by courses in the history of political thought have been considered, but only as far as they are concerned with the topic to be examined.

The principal goal of this study is to provide an analytic interpretation and a critical understanding of different political philosophies dealing with the same problem. I have tried to give each of them a fair hearing; but I have not felt compelled to confine myself to a strict—and bland—neutrality. I am convinced that only one of these alternative views is correct, and I have stated my criticisms of all others. In this way, the study might most effectively fulfill its most important purpose, to stimulate discussion. It should therefore be no less useful to those who disagree than to those who will be convinced by the arguments—or who do not need to be.

Finding myself between two chairs, political science and philosophy, I was fortunate to benefit from the help of colleagues sitting firmly on one or the other. George Kateb and Michael Walzer in political science and Elizabeth and Monroe Beardsley, Hugo Bedau and Carl Hempel in philosophy read the whole manuscript in draft form and gave many creative suggestions. My deepest thanks go to each of them, as well as to Gregory Fahlund, a graduate student who worked on the preparation of the manuscript. The help is theirs, the shortcomings are mine.

Amherst, Massachusetts   **Felix E. Oppenheim**
May 15, 1967

Contents

A Note on Citations

For the purpose of a critical analysis of moral philosophies propounded by various political thinkers, it seemed better to refer to their own words as far as possible rather than to paraphrase their ideas. Hence the relatively large number of quotations. To avoid footnotes, sources are indicated after each passage quoted. And to avoid encumbering the text, certain abbreviations have been used. Classical writers, from Plato to Herbert Spencer, are quoted by title (sometimes abbreviated), book (large Roman numerals), chapter (small Roman numerals), and/or section or paragraph (arabic numerals), as the case may be. This will enable readers using various editions to find the quoted passage. Whenever possible, the most readily available editions have been used in this study. More recent publications are quoted by author and page number (but not by title); the year of publication is indicated when more than one work by the same author is quoted. Throughout, numerals without other indications refer to the last work quoted. The *List of Works Cited* indicates full titles, editions used, and acknowledgments of permission to reprint. Italics are in the original, unless otherwise indicated.

Moral Principles

in Political Philosophy

1

Political Science, Political Ethics, Political Philosophy

"Any individual has the moral right and even duty to engage in acts of civil disobedience as a protest against laws or policies which he considers clearly immoral, such as racial discrimination or certain military operations." "No, citizens have the moral obligation to obey even those measures which they deem unjust, especially in a democracy which provides institutional devices for the peaceful change of laws and policies."

When such a typical ethical disagreement comes up, the first impulse is to take sides—to come to the rescue of one or the other of the contestants, either by voicing agreement, or by appealing to some respected authority, or by pointing out that adopting the opponent's attitude leads to consequences of which he himself is likely to disapprove.

One may, however, raise the debate to a higher level of abstraction and ask: Is it possible to *demonstrate* that the moral judgment of either one or the other is correct, and hence that of his opponent mistaken? Are there universal principles by which to assess the truth of *any* judgment of political morality? If there are, we would have to subscribe to whichever principle turns out to be true, regardless of our subjective preferences, just as we have no choice but to accept the uncomfortable factual truth that no cure for cancer has as yet been found. If, on the other hand, there are no objective foundations for politically relevant principles of morality, further questions arise: Is the adoption of one or the other of two conflicting systems of political ethics merely a matter of subjective value commitment? If so, does it follow that inductive and deductive reasoning play no role at all in the adoption of political principles, the choice of political goals, the verdicts of political judgment?

Such questions, and the various answers given to them, have been a recurrent theme throughout the history of political thought and will be the exclusive topic of this study. It will not advocate any normative doctrine, ideology, or principle of politics. It will not *make* political value judgments but speak *about* them. It belongs not to political ethics but to political philosophy.

Our topic, so conceived, is based on the fundamental distinction between moral principles of politics which make up the discipline of political ethics and statements about such moral principles which belong to political philosophy. Political ethics, however, must not only be distinguished from political philosophy; both political philosophy and political ethics should also be set off from political science. Let us establish the latter distinction first.

I *Political Science*

a / SCIENCE IN GENERAL

Any science is an organized body of knowledge about some given subject matter. The purpose of science is not merely to describe observed or otherwise known phenomena but to explain them and possibly to predict future events. Both explanations and predictions involve reliance upon general laws. The discovery of general laws is therefore the fundamental task of every science. Why this pot of water bubbles now can be explained with the help of the general law that water boils at 100° C. (and the particular statement that this pot has been heated to that temperature). The same law enables us to predict that the pot, if heated to 100°, will boil. Similarly, the law that the price of goods increases if the supply of goods diminishes makes it possible to explain and to predict a great number of particular economic phenomena.

This general characterization of science is in some respects broader and in other respects narrower than certain other definitions currently in use. In most contemporary writings, science is linked with the "scientific method," which appraises the acceptability of statements concerning our world by means of relevant empirical evidence, such as observational findings or experimental tests. According to this view, a statement is scientific if, and only if, it is at least in principle and however indirectly, empirically testable. Accordingly, statements which assert that something is red or that some action constitutes larceny would be scientific, and so would assertions about atoms, cells, the subconscious, inflation, or political authority, but not statements referring to Rousseau's "general will" or Hegel's "world spirit." Yet many thinkers, especially in the past and especially when dealing with social matters, have used different methods to arrive at and to support their generalizations; e.g., Platonic intuition, Thomistic teleology, Hegelian dialectic. While denying that observation is a source, or the only source, of reliable knowledge, they do not deny the possibility of discovering general laws by nonempirical and yet objective methods, nor the possibility of explaining and even predicting particular events by virtue of those generalizations which they claim to have discovered. Their writings deserve to be considered scientific in a broad sense, though this cannot be done if we identify science with the "scientific method." The question whether this method is applicable to the study of human behavior in general and to political phenomena in particular is still alive and cannot be settled simply by definition.

Just as there are descriptive generalizations, so is it possible to formulate normative principles. Accordingly, science is sometimes taken to include not only factual investigations but ethical generalizations as well. Furthermore, it has often been held, rightly or wrongly, that moral principles can be empirically tested just like descriptive laws of physics or of human behavior, and that ethics constitutes, therefore, a science even in the narrow sense. To speak of ethics as a science would, however, blur the distinction, fundamental for the purposes of this study, between those statements, judgments, laws, principles, or theories which are *descriptive* or factual and those which are normative or ethical. I shall, therefore, allot to the language of science only descriptive statements, whether they "describe" some particular state of affairs or assert some general "descriptive law."

b / POLITICAL SCIENCE IN PARTICULAR

Little needs to be said about how to distinguish politics as a subject matter of science from other fields of inquiry. Politics has to do with human behavior and more precisely with human interaction. There is no exact boundary between political and other interaction relationships, and it is enough to say that "political relationship in some way involves authority, ruling, or power." (Dahl, p. 5) The science of politics therefore consists of descriptive statements about political phenomena. Like every science, it aims at explaining, if not at predicting, political events by virtue of general descriptive laws or principles, which may be more or less strictly political but are often borrowed from other sciences such as psychology, sociology, economics, or even the natural sciences. Political science has traditionally been concerned with such topics as: "human nature" in politics, the origin and nature of political authority, the causes of political conflicts and their resolution by authoritative decision or by mutual accommodation.

Here are, chosen at random from the writings of classical political thinkers, some descriptive generalizations which were meant to serve as bases for the explanation of particular political events. They belong to political science in our sense of the term, regardless of whether their authors considered them to be empirically warranted or true on some other grounds, and regardless, of course, of whether or not contemporary political scientists consider them tenable. "In every case the laws are made by the ruling party in its own interest." (Thrasymachus in Plato, *Republic*, 338) "It is evident that the polis belongs to the class of things that exist by nature, and that man is by nature an animal intended to live in a polis." (Aristotle, *Politics*, 1253a) "Nature hath made men so equal, in the faculties of the body, and mind . . . ." (Hobbes, *Leviathan*, xiii) "Man is born free; and everywhere he is in chains." (Rousseau, *Social Contract*, I, i) "Nature has placed mankind under the governance of two sovereign masters, *pain* and *pleasure*." (Bentham, *Principles*, i, 1) "The history of all hitherto existing society is the history of class struggles." (Marx, *Communist Manifesto*)

II *Political Ethics*

I have dealt with the general features of science and political science in particular only for the purpose of distinguishing them from ethics and political ethics which are more closely related to the subject matter of this study.

a / SCIENCE AND ETHICS

While science tries to explain what is or to predict what will be, ethics seeks to determine what ought to be done. Like science, ethics is primarily interested in the formulation of general principles, under which particular cases may be subsumed. For example, the ethical principle of utility which holds that "actions are right in proportion as they tend to promote happiness" (Mill, *Utilitarianism*, ii) is meant to serve as a guide to any particular action in every circumstance. Ethics, then, determines and recommends the adoption of certain general principles or rules or standards or ideals of conduct. Psychological, sociological, or political explanations of why certain individuals or groups subscribe to certain moral principles belong to descriptive science, not to normative ethics. The concept of ethics is unduly enlarged if it is made to include such factual investigations, just as the notion of science becomes too broad if it is taken to comprise ethics. The questions whether and how ethical principles can be justified do not belong to normative ethics either but to analytic philosophy, as we shall see.

b / MORAL JUDGMENTS AND VALUE JUDGMENTS

While science consists only of descriptive statements, ethics includes moral and value statements as well. There are several types of moral statements or judgments, but we shall be concerned only with assertions to the effect that a certain action or kind of action is morally right or wrong, just or unjust, or that one is obligated to do or to avoid doing it. A value judgment, on the other hand, states that a certain object or kind of object or state of affairs is good or bad, beautiful or ugly, desirable or undesirable or preferable to some other.* The language of ethics may include not only moral judgments as to what actions are right but also value judgments as to what things are good. However, some value judgments are outside ethics. To determine that a painting is beautiful is to make an esthetic judgment, a nonmoral value judgment. To enter the purview of ethics, a value judgment must pertain to some state of affairs which does or can come about as a result of human action.

According to many moralists, the rightness of an action depends on the value of its consequences (either actual or probable or intended): any actor ought to perform that action among the alternatives open to him in any given situation which would have the best possible outcome on the whole. According to this view, "the basic or ultimate criterion or standard of what is morally right, wrong, obligatory, etc., is . . . the comparative balance of good over evil produced." (Frankena, 1963, p. 13) Then, the value judgment that a certain state of affairs is the best possible is part of the language of morals. For example, Mill's value judgment that "pleasure, and freedom from pain, are the only things desirable as ends" is ethical in character, since he links it to the ethical norm that "actions are right in proportion as they tend to promote . . . pleasure, and the absence of pain." (Mill, *Utilitarianism*, ii) †

* The term 'value judgment' is often used in a broader sense to include moral judgments as well as value judgments in the narrower sense.

† This so-called teleological theory (from the Greek 'telos', meaning 'end') must be distinguished from deontological ethical theories, according to which the rightness of an action depends on some of its formal properties, regardless of its consequences; e.g., the principle that telling the truth is obligatory under all circum-

c / INTRINSIC AND EXTRINSIC VALUE JUDGMENTS

A distinction is usually made between intrinsic and extrinsic value judgments. Intrinsic value judgments state that something is good or bad in itself or is intrinsically preferable to something else. For example, someone might hold that freedom of speech is intrinsically valuable or desirable, and that its restriction is intrinsically disvaluable or undesirable. Extrinsic value judgments assert that a thing is good because it is conducive to something else: freedom of speech is good because it promotes knowledge; its restriction is good for the sake of protecting national security. These examples show that something (freedom of speech) may be considered valuable both intrinsically and extrinsically, and that something (e.g., restricting freedom of speech) may be deemed intrinsically disvaluable but extrinsically valuable.

Moral judgments, too, may be said to be either intrinsic or extrinsic according to whether they stipulate that something (e.g., protecting freedom of speech) ought to be done for its own sake or for the sake of some other goal. Now, the statement that restricting freedom of speech is desirable for the sake of protecting national security means the same as: *if* national security is to be protected, *then* freedom of speech must be limited (in certain areas); or: such limitations are a necessary *means* to the end of protecting national security. Instrumental value judgments can always be translated without loss of meaning into 'if-then' or 'means-end' statements which contain no value words like 'good' or moral terms like 'ought'. Thus they are purely descriptive and hence ethically neutral; they belong as such to science, not to ethics. Strictly speaking, the language of ethics includes only genuine (i.e., intrinsic) valuational

---

stances. A strictly deontological system of ethics would consist only of moral principles and contain no judgments as to the value of an action's consequences.

and moral judgments. In practice, however, questions of means are often so intricately linked with considerations of ends that the border line between science and ethics cannot always be drawn with precision.

Principles of right action and of desirable outcomes can be applied only to human individuals and only to the extent to which they have a choice between alternative courses of action. There is an important school of thought, however, ranging from Aristotle via Aquinas to modern Thomism, which considers not only man but the whole of nature to be purposeful and tending toward its "end, or final cause, [which] is the best." (Aristotle, *Politics*, 1253a) We shall see later that these thinkers implicitly deny the distinction between fact and value, descriptive and normative principles, science and ethics.

d / ETHICS AND POLITICAL ETHICS

Political ethics is particularly concerned with determining how men ought to act in their capacity as citizens or government officials, especially legislators. Most political thinkers hold that the rightness of political actions depends essentially on the desirability of the consequences and that it is to a large extent within the power of political actors to bring about and to preserve desirable political systems. Value judgments about the good society are therefore as important a part of political ethics as are normative judgments about right political behavior.* Some of the perennial issues in the his-

---

* These generalizations must be qualified. A minority of political thinkers have adopted deontological rather than teleological standards of political morality; e.g., the rule that obeying positive law is a moral duty under any circumstances, regardless of political consequences. Strict determinists or fatalists such as St. Augustine and Marx deny that deliberate individual choice and action can influence and modify the inevitable course of political events. According to the former view, political ethics includes only normative but no value judgments; according to the latter, there can be, strictly speaking, no political ethics.

tory of political ethics are individual freedom versus
governmental control; egalitarianism versus elitism; political obligation to obey governmental authority versus
the right of resistance; individual welfare versus national glory. Taking a side on such issues requires appeal
to some *moral* principle of politics. To say this, however, does not imply that one morally approves of the
principles. Statements to the effect that slavery or racial
discrimination or censorship is wrong express principles of political ethics; but so do the judgments that
such policies are desirable. In this sense (and throughout this study) the word 'moral' is used in contradistinction not to 'immoral' but to 'factual'.

e / POLITICAL ETHICS AND POLITICAL SCIENCE

Theoretically, the language of political ethics comprises
only intrinsic ethical and valuational statements, while
extrinsic moral and value judgments fall within the
scope of political science, or what has been more recently called "the policy sciences." For example, Machiavelli's *The Prince* is essentially a catalogue of rules
of rationality such as, "In taking a state the conqueror
must arrange to commit all his cruelties at once." (viii)
It is the classical example of an ethically neutral inquiry
into the most effective means to reach a certain goal
(the wielding of absolute power) without concern for
the question of the intrinsic desirability of the goal itself.

However, few political writings of the past and even
of the present consist exclusively of either descriptive
generalizations including instrumental value judgments
or of intrinsic moral or valuational principles. Most political thinkers are concerned with determining the
means to those goals to which they themselves attach
positive intrinsic value, and thus their writings contain
elements of both political science and political ethics.
For instance:

Whoever has the legislative or supreme power of any commonwealth is bound to govern by established standing laws, promulgated and known to the people, and not by extemporary decrees; . . . . And all this to be directed to no other end but the peace, safety, and public good of the people. (Locke, *Civil Government*, 131)

Here it might seem artificial to assign the intrinsic moral principle that government ought to secure peace, security, and the public good to political ethics and the affirmation that this goal can be achieved only through "government under law" to political science. Concrete policies are connected with ultimate political goals by long means-end chains, and political ethics may well be construed as comprising all of the more remote links.

Keeping these qualifications in mind, here are, again chosen from the writings of classical thinkers, some moral principles of politics which may be clearly recognized as such because they either contain ethical or valuational terms (italicized here) or are couched in the imperative mood. "It is clear . . . that the *best* form of political society is one where power is vested in the middle class." (Aristotle, *Politics*, 1295b) "Whoever our governors are, they *ought* to possess our esteem and veneration." (Calvin, *Institutes*, IV, xx, 22) "The *end* of government is the good of mankind." (Locke, *Civil Government*, 229; see also his statement quoted above) "Laws and social arrangements *should* place the happiness, . . . of every individual, as nearly as possible in harmony with the interest of the whole." (Mill, *Utilitarianism*, ii; see also his statement quoted above) "Workingmen of all countries unite!" (Marx, *Communist Manifesto*)

However, political writers often sacrifice logical precision to rhetorical effectiveness, using apparently descriptive statements to express norms of political ethics. For example, Locke's statement that "he that cannot take away his own life, cannot give another power over it" (*Civil Government*, 23) is obviously a more forceful way of expressing this moral rule than by saying that nobody *ought* to take his own life, let alone give someone else power over it. Similarly, Rousseau expresses the moral judgment that legislative power ought to belong to the people by means of the apparently factual assertion that "legislative power belongs to the people, and can belong to it alone." (*Social Contract*, III, i) That all men are equal may have declarative or normative meaning, depending on the context. If the former, it means that men *have* certain properties in common; if the latter, that men *ought* to be allotted the same benefits or burdens (e.g., equal rights).

The use of persuasive definitions is another rhetorical device frequently used by political writers to express their moral views. For example, 'freedom' can be defined in terms of certain interaction relationships and used as a descriptive term in political science. But, because of its laudatory connotation, this word tends to be utilized by political philosophers to refer to those, and only those, situations which they happen to value positively. (To this point, see Oppenheim, 1961, pp. 155–172.) Thus when Rousseau states that "obedience to a law which we prescribe to ourselves is liberty" (*Social Contract*, I, viii), he does not mean to define the concept of freedom; he is stipulating that citizens ought to obey only those laws which emanate from "themselves," i.e., from "the general will." Similarly, to say that "democracy is . . . the good society itself in operation" (Lipset, p. 403) is to recommend democracy by means of a statement intended to be an ethically neutral definition.

These examples show not only why it is often very difficult but also why it is very important to distinguish between descriptive and normative aspects when dealing with political writings.

III *Analytic Political Philosophy*

There are as many definitions of 'philosophy' as there are philosophers. This difficulty has no bearing on the present study which is concerned only with one branch of philosophy, namely analytic philosophy or philosophy of science. Since we are confining the term 'science' to descriptive science in contradistinction to ethics, we shall make the corresponding distinction between philosophy of science and philosophy of ethics.

1 / Philosophy of Political Science

Unlike the various sciences which have as their subject matter physical or biological or psychological or social phenomena, philosophy of science does not presume to add to our factual knowledge of the "real world" but aims rather at increasing a critical understanding of the body of knowledge which the former are providing. Philosophy of science deals not with the subject matter of the various sciences but with the *statements* the sciences make about their respective subject matters; e.g., the ways these statements are determined, tested, explained and justified.

Philosophy of political science deals with the logical analysis of descriptive concepts, particular statements, and general hypotheses about political phenomena. The clarification of such basic terms as 'political power', 'authority', 'sovereignty', 'freedom', 'equality', and those referring to various political institutions and forms of government has always been of foremost concern to political thinkers, and the question whether these rather abstract words can be defined by (however indirect) reference to observable properties and relations is still an open one. No less controversial and important is the other main problem of the philosophy of political science—whether descriptive knowledge about politics is to be gained by the empirical method generally adopted by the natural sciences or whether the understanding of political behavior (and of human conduct generally) requires quite different methods such as ones employing *a priori* "reason" or empathic "insight." This question is connected with the epistemological controversy between those who affirm and those who deny the possibility of "value-free" (i.e., objective) research in the area of politics.

2 / Philosophy of Political Ethics

Philosophy of ethics is related to ethics as philosophy of science is to science. This part of analytic philosophy is also called *metaethics,* in contradistinction to normative ethics. (The term 'ethics' is sometimes used to refer to metaethics as well as to normative ethics, a fact which makes for confusion.) Metaethical assertions are, like those of philosophy of science, neither descriptive nor normative but philosophical. "In short, metaethics consists, not in making moral statements, but in making statements *about* moral statements; not in moral reasoning, but in reasoning *about* moral reasoning." (Taylor, pp. xi–xii) The two most important problems of metaethics concern (1) the meaning of value words such as 'good' or 'preferable' and moral terms such as 'right' and 'duty'; and (2) the logic of moral discourse: Are moral principles objectively either true or false? If they are, by what method can such principles be justified? Although we shall be primarily interested in the second problem, the first question concerns us also because one's interpretation of valuational and ethical concepts necessarily determines one's position as to whether and how ethical principles can be shown to be true or false.

The distinctions made so far are necessary to delimit the domain of what will be the topic of this study, namely, philosophy of political ethics. The title

"Moral Principles in Political Philosophy," is meant to indicate that the study deals with moral principles of politics, not directly, but as an object of philosophical analysis. More precise, but also more forbidding, titles would have been: "Metaethics of Politics" or "Philosophies of Political Ethics"—'philosophies' in the plural, as I shall examine alternative philosophical views about moral principles of politics which have been proposed by some of the most influential political philosophers.

Metaethics of politics does not itself propound moral principles but makes statements *about* them—their meaning, function, and justification. However, not all assertions about moral judgments of politics belong to philosophy of political ethics. The history, sociology, and psychology of political thought also have something to say about statements of political ethics—and of political science as well. These disciplines, however, deal with them from a descriptive-factual, not a philosophical-analytical, point of view. They may either describe, for example, that Locke advocated limited government (i.e., that he subscribed to the view that limited government is desirable), or explain why he held this view (by reference to political events such as the Glorious Revolution), or establish causal connections between the doctrine of limited government and antecedent or subsequent political ideas or events. We have seen that the task of explaining why a certain political theory has been adopted belongs to political science, not to political ethics, and not, we may now add, to political philosophy either. Unlike the political moralist who tries to convince us that we should adhere to some specific political doctrine and act accordingly, the philosopher of political ethics carries out his investigation from an ethically neutral point of view, like the philosopher of political science and the political scientist, including the historian of political thought.

We have already dealt with a metaethical problem of politics; namely, how to determine whether a given statement about political matters belongs to political science or to political ethics. A related question, and again one which falls within the purview of metaethics, concerns the distinction between the ethical and meta-ethical statements of politics. It has been pointed out that typical political writings are seldom either completely factual or exclusively valuational. Nor do they ever confine themselves to purely methodological considerations without any concern for substantive political issues. Political thinkers are unlikely to have an abstract interest in the logical structure of principles of political morality in general. They are committed to some specific political doctrine and may raise the questions whether and how their own moral principles can be justified.

Most political philosophers are also, and in most cases primarily, social critics and reformers; and their interest in metaethical issues is often incidental. For example: "We hold these Truths to be self-evident, that all Men . . . are endowed by their Creator with certain unalienable Rights. . . . That to secure these Rights, Governments are instituted among Men." Clearly, the framers of the Declaration of Independence meant, first of all, to propound the moral rule that governments ought to secure these rights; in the second place, to claim that these particular moral "truths" are "self-evident"; and in the third place, to affirm the general principle that there are self-evident norms of political ethics. The second and third claims are metaethical, while the first is normative. Most political writings constitute a mixture—often indiscriminate—of factual, ethical, and sometimes also epistemological considerations; it is nevertheless possible, and also necessary, to separate these elements.

Henceforth I shall concentrate on what remains the most important, and also the most controversial, issue of metaethics in general and of the philosophy of political ethics in particular: Is the adoption of any given

moral principle an expression of subjective commitment, or can such principles, or their denial, be shown
to be objectively true, and if so how? On this issue, political thinkers have been profoundly divided, and their
metaethical disagreements often cut across ethical and
ideological alignments. For example, there is at least one,
if rather general, principle of political ethics to which
Aristotle, Aquinas, Locke, Hume, Rousseau, Bentham,
and Niebuhr are equally committed; namely, that political institutions and policies should ultimately serve to
promote the citizen's well-being (whereas Plato, Augustine, Burke, Spencer, modern nationalists and totalitari-
ans advocate different ultimate political goals). Yet
some of these thinkers deny, while others affirm, that
this principle can be objectively justified, and the latter
differ among one another as to the method of justification. On the other hand, two thinkers such as Rousseau
and Burke may hold the same metaethical view;
namely, that certain basic principles of political ethics
can be apprehended through intuitive moral insight but
differ as to the content of these very principles which
both claim to be objectively true, and true on the same
grounds. Students of political theory have tended to
focus their attention on the ethical rather than on the
metaethical level. Yet philosophical issues of political
ethics are not only of theoretical interest but also of
political significance. It seems therefore worthwhile to
attempt a systematic and critical examination of the
various answers which have been given to the most
basic question of political philosophy.

2

Philosophies of Political Ethics

I *Value-cognitivism and Its Denial*

The various and conflicting theories which have been advanced in answer to the question whether or not valuational and ethical principles are a matter of knowledge have been classified into value-cognitivism and value-noncognitivism, and the former metaethical theory has been subdivided into intuitionism and naturalism. Like the general distinction between ethics and metaethics, these categories are of fairly recent vintage. Since they have proven to be convenient and effective analytical tools, I shall apply them later to various political philosophies of the past as well as of the present. In this chapter I shall merely give a brief explication of these alternative metaethical theories.

1 / Value-cognitivism

The metaethical theory of value-cognitivism affirms that valuational and moral statements are assertions about objective states of affairs and have, as such, cognitive status; that is, they are, and can be known to be, either true or false. Thus, value-cognitivists consider the moral principle: 'segregation is wrong' to be as objectively true or false as the factual statement: 'segregation is considered morally right in South Africa'. And just as the factual statement: 'segregation is practiced in South Africa' is true if, and only if, South Africa does practice segregation, so the ethical statement: 'segregation is wrong' is considered true, provided policies which are segregational also have the characteristic of being morally wrong.

This is not to say that all cognitivists regard moral principles to be true on the same grounds as empirical statements. Some hold certain moral principles to be necessarily true, in the manner of mathematical truths. Others consider them true for still other reasons.

Cognitivism thus interprets ethical terms as standing for objectively ascertainable characteristics of actions or of outcomes of actions.* Accordingly, an act or kind of act may have the quality of being either right or wrong, and its outcome the characteristic of being either good or bad, just as some object either has or lacks the property of being yellow or solid or cold. Ethical properties can be apprehended (whether by sense experience or in some other way) just like physical properties. This is what Aristotle meant when he spoke of the "*perception of good and evil, . . . and other similar qualities.*" (*Politics*, 1253a; italics added)

The philosophy of value-cognitivism in politics holds

---

* We can see here how the problem of the cognitive status of moral statements depends upon some assumption about the meaning of moral concepts.

that certain political institutions and policies have the objective quality of being either good or bad, right or wrong; that there are objective criteria by which to determine whether a given political system is or is not good or right; that such normative principles of political ethics can be known, just as one can know descriptive laws of political behavior. To quote a contemporary cognitivist political philosopher:

All political action is then guided by some thought of better and worse. But thought of better or worse implies thought of the good . . . . The very fact that we can question it directs us towards such a thought of the good as is no longer questionable—towards a thought which is no longer opinion but knowledge. All political action has then in itself a directedness towards knowledge of the good; of the good life, or the good society . . . . Political philosophy is the attempt truly *to know* both the nature of political things and *the right, or the good, political order.* (Strauss, 1959, pp. 10, 12; italics added)

The question *how* the quality of goodness in general and of political goodness in particular can be known is answered differently by the two schools of cognitivism, intuitionism and naturalism.

a / NATURALISM

Of the two cognitivist theories, naturalism is at present the more widely accepted. Naturalism in general holds that certain moral principles can be shown to be true by reducing them somehow to true descriptive generalizations. According to a great number of political thinkers, ethical judgments *follow* from nonmoral (empirical or teleological) statements, as we shall see.

In contrast to this simpler form of naturalism, there is a more sophisticated version according to which certain valuational or moral terms can be *defined* by nonvaluational and nonmoral expressions. For example, 'good' means the same as: 'what is conducive to pleasure'. Given this definition, and given the fact that such and such a state of affairs is conducive to pleasure, it follows (so the argument goes) that such a state of affairs is good. The concept of goodness or rightness has also been defined by reference to subjective feelings, either of the majority or of "experts" or of the speaker himself. For example, if 'morally wrong' is synonymous with 'disapproved by most', and if it is true that segregation is disapproved by most, then it is also true that segregation is morally wrong.

Except for those who use the teleological approach, naturalists consider certain basic ethical principles to be empirically true because they can be, if not directly observed, derived from empirical generalizations, either with or without the help of naturalistic definitions of ethical concepts. If naturalism is correct, then ethics is an empirical science.

b / INTUITIONISM

Intuitionists agree with naturalists that ethical terms refer to objective characteristics, but interpret them as designating "nonnatural" or "simple" properties which cannot be further defined. Thus G. E. Moore, the most influential of modern intuitionists, makes the point that

'good' is a simple notion, just as 'yellow' is a simple notion; that just as you cannot, by any manner of means, explain to anyone who does not already know it, what yellow is, so you cannot explain what good is. (Moore, p. 7)

Many intuitionists hold that the quality of goodness or rightness, unlike the property of being yellow, cannot be perceived by sense experience but instead is known by moral insight. Men are endowed with a moral sense which is as capable of apprehending moral qualities as the five senses are in perceiving physical properties. If intuition reveals that segregation is evil, then the statement: 'segregation is evil' is true, and anyone who denies this moral truth is "value blind" and as much in error as a color-blind person who mistakes a red light for a green one. Other intuitionists consider religious revelation a valid ground for holding certain moral principles to be true. According to both these views, true moral principles are *synthetic a priori*: synthetic because they can be denied without self-contradiction (e.g., it is not self-contradictory to deny that segregation is evil); *a priori* because they are true independently of sense experience.

According to a related view, certain basic ethical norms are true *a priori* because they are necessarily true, like the principle of logic that a thing cannot at the same time have and lack a certain property. Those who hold that some moral truths are self-evident fall within this category. Such philosophers do not base moral principles on moral intuition or religious faith. They may nevertheless be classified as intuitionists in a larger sense since they claim that there are fundamental moral principles which can be known to be true on the basis of rational, rather than moral or religious, insight.

2 / Value-noncognitivism

Value-noncognitivism as a metaethical theory may be summarized as follows: Basic ethical principles have no cognitive status; they cannot be *known* to be either true or false because they *are* not true or false; and they are neither true nor false because they do not affirm or deny that something is the case.

Grammatically, 'patriotism is a virtue' is a declarative sentence, just like 'John approves of patriotism' or 'Jack is patriotic'. But on closer scrutiny this appearance is deceptive. Such judgments do not have the function of conveying information about matters of fact; they serve a different purpose, namely, that of *expressing* valuational and normative attitudes. When A says that patriotism is a virtue, he does not assign the property of being virtuous to patriotism but conveys his *approval* of patriotic actions and expresses the ethical judgment that one ought to act in a patriotic way. And he implicitly enjoins others to adopt the same moral attitude and to act accordingly. If B replies that patriotism is bad, he does not thereby contradict A's statement but merely expresses his own, different, moral evaluation of patriotism. The disagreement between A and B is thus a "disagreement in attitude" which may subsist even if there is no "disagreement in belief." * Indeed, A and B may agree on all the relevant facts and still take opposite moral attitudes toward patriotism.

There are no arguments, whether intuitionistic or naturalistic, by which either A's or B's moral point of view can be shown to be true. Subjective moral commitments cannot be objectively justified. In the words of one of the most influential modern exponents of this view:

In saying that a certain type of action is right or wrong, I am not making any factual statement, not even a statement about my own state of mind. I am merely expressing certain moral sentiments . . . . If a sentence makes no statement at all, there is obviously no sense in asking whether what it says is true or false. (Ayer, pp. 107–108)

A sentence of the type: 'This action is morally right or good' "makes no statement at all" because a term of the type 'good' in the moral sense designates no property at all which an action may either have or lack.

This is not to deny that 'good' in the nonmoral sense does have descriptive meaning. Disagreement between A and B as to whether a car is good is a disagreement as to how it rates with respect to road performance, gas and oil consumption, etc. In certain contexts, the function of the word 'good' is both descriptive and expressive. By calling an income tax law good, A expresses his

* This distinction was first made by Stevenson; see especially chapters 1 and 2.

approval of this law by virtue of its having certain descriptive features, e.g., that it reduces differences in net income, that it effectively raises tax revenue, etc. B may consider the same law bad, either because he disagrees with A as to its characteristics or because he disapproves of them. On the other hand, when A says that freedom of expression is intrinsically good and desirable, there is no descriptive feature of freedom of expression to which he refers, even implicitly. If B disagrees with A, their disagreement is exclusively one of attitude toward freedom of expression.* Fundamental moral disputes cannot be resolved in any objective way, and fundamental moral claims cannot be inductively established or deductively proven or demonstrated in any other way. Morality is not a matter of knowledge.

There is one point on which noncognitivism agrees with cognitivism of the *intuitionistic* variety, namely, that words like 'good' and 'right' are undefinable; not, however, because they designate "simple properties" but because they do not designate anything at all. Some may find it more difficult to distinguish noncognitivism from the variety of *naturalism* which holds that 'x is good' is a synonym of: 'x is preferred by the speaker A'. According to both theories, valuational concepts are not like property terms such as 'yellow' or 'pleasurable' but like relational terms such as 'larger than'. Value terms refer to relationships of subjective preference which hold between the speaker and a certain kind of action or state of affairs. Yet there is a crucial difference. According to the naturalistic view, A's statement: 'patriotism is a virtue' *means* the same as: 'A approves of patriotism'; consequently, A's value judgment that pa-

---

* Their disagreement would be factual if the question were whether freedom of expression is good or bad not intrinsically but as a means to a commonly agreed end, e.g., that government ought to promote the greatest happiness of the greatest number. Value-noncognitivists do not deny that such extrinsic value judgments are either true or false. This point will be taken up in the next section.

triotism is a virtue is objectively true if A approves of patriotism and false if he in fact disapproves of patriotism but for some reason wants others to believe that he admires it. Noncognitivism claims that such an ethical judgment does not convey information, either about patriotism or about A, but *expresses* A's approval of patriotism. "*Expressing* a feeling is not to be confused with *asserting* that one has it. Assertions about feelings are statements, and as such true or false." (Beardsley and Beardsley, p. 530) *Expressions* of feelings are not statements at all, hence cannot be either true or false. This is the noncognitivist position.

Value-noncognitivism has also been called emotivism because the most popular version of this theory holds that ethical judgments merely express the speaker's emotions.

In every case in which one would commonly be said to be making an ethical judgment, the function of the relevant ethical word is purely "emotive." It is used to express feelings about certain objects, but not to make any assertion about them. (Ayer, p. 108)

More recently, noncognitivism has shifted the emphasis from the emotive to the prescriptive aspect of ethical language. According to this view, moral rules are propounded not so much to express the speaker's "emotions" as to influence his listener to adopt similar attitudes. A representative spokesman for this imperative theory holds

that the primary function of the word 'good' is to commend . . . . When we commend' or condemn anything, it is always in order, at least indirectly, to guide choices, our own or other people's, now or in the future. (Hare, 1952, p. 127)

This interpretation clearly brings out the dynamic, interpersonal, and social function of ethical discourse.

Furthermore, the emotive theory makes it appear as if espousing some general moral principle were simply a matter of unreflective, and perhaps transitory, taste, like deciding between chocolate or vanilla ice cream. The prescriptivist theory stresses an important point to which I shall return in a moment. While denying that basic moral principles can be said to be true or false, valid or nonvalid, correct or incorrect, noncognitivism does not question the possibility of determining whether the adoption of such principles is rationally justified.

3 / Relevance of this Controversy

The issue between cognitivism and noncognitivism does not pertain to all valuational and moral statements. In connection with political ethics, it is especially important to distinguish between normative statements falling within the scope of this controversy and those outside.

a / JUDGMENTS OF RATIONALITY

Both cognitivists and noncognitivists agree that judgments of rationality do have cognitive status. Judgments of rationality concern the adequacy of the choice of a course of action or policy in view of attaining a desired state of affairs, judged on the basis of the information available to an actor in a given situation. Questions of rationality must be settled on the basis of empirical and logical considerations, not on moral grounds.*

Whether the recommended course of action constitutes an effective means to a given end is just one test of its rationality. As pointed out, so-called instrumental value judgments are actually empirical statements.

---

* Adhering to a certain code of morality may, of course, itself be considered rational in view of the pursuit of some ulterior goal. Morality may be the best policy. On the other hand, acting rationally may itself be considered morally right, as does the ethics of "enlightened" self-interest.

Consequently, all of the "policy sciences" remain unaffected by the issue of value-cognitivism versus value-noncognitivism. Policy sciences may deal with the rationality not only of the most immediate political actions but also of intermediate goals with respect to some ultimate end. For example, according to J. S. Mill freedom of opinion is a necessary condition of, and hence a necessary means to, the promotion of truth; and since "no belief which is contrary to truth can be really useful" (*On Liberty*, ii), promoting truth is in turn conducive to general happiness. Another means-end chain leads from freedom of opinion to "individual spontaneity," from there to the development of "persons of genius" (*On Liberty*, iii), and again to general happiness. Whether these causal links hold is, in principle, an empirical matter. It is true, however, that Mill values each of these intermediate goals not only extrinsically but also intrinsically, like the ultimate goal of general happiness. Here the question does arise whether it can be demonstrated that each of these states of affairs is desirable in itself.

Some questions of rationality can be answered by reference to attainability. This problem is of special importance in the political sphere. Utopianism in the sense of advocating or trying to pursue some goal which, on the basis of the available evidence, cannot be reached by whatever means is an instance of irrational behavior. Whether Plato's rule by the best in the common interest or Marx's classless society is utopian or not is again a question of fact. If these goals *are* utopian, then there is no point of even raising the further question of their desirability.

The simultaneous advocacy of specific ends which are not just competing but actually conflicting is perhaps the most common instance of irrationality in politics. Policy-makers are, of course, especially prone to wanting to have their cake and eat it too. A government may advocate, and even attempt to pursue simultaneously, a

foreign policy that includes promoting the independence of other countries and hence opposing intervention in their domestic affairs; strengthening "free" governments and thus accepting intervention for such
purposes; and protecting its own national security and
hence allowing foreign intervention if, and only if, required for that purpose. Whether these three goals are
incompatible and whether it is, therefore, irrational to
adopt them all is surely a matter of fact, not of morality.*

Theoretical systems of political ethics, too, give rise
to the question: Do they meet this criterion of rationality? Is Calvin's injunction "even to submit to the government of all who possess the sovereignty, even though
they perform none of the duties of their function" (*Institutes*, IV, xx, 29) empirically, or even logically, compatible with his other prescription that "if they command anything against him [the Lord], it ought not to
have the least attention; nor, in this case, ought we to
pay any regard to all that dignity attached to magis-
trates"? (*Ibid.*, 32) † Is it consistent to assign to government the task both of maximizing total utility or
"happiness" or welfare *and* of providing for its equal
distribution, as do many utilitarians, at least implicitly?
Is freedom for all compatible with happiness for all?
Bentham implicitly answers this question affirmatively
and Dostoyevsky's Grand Inquisitor negatively. The
point I wish to make here is that answers to such questions are pertinent to the rationality and not the morality of political behavior. The cognitivist-noncognitivist
debate is, therefore, not relevant here.

---

* *Pursuing* the third goal may, of course, be compatible with
advocating the first or the second for propaganda purposes.

† If to "command anything against the Lord" does constitute a
failure to perform a "duty of their function," the two prescriptions
are logically incompatible; otherwise, they are compatible.

b / DERIVED ETHICAL PRINCIPLES

A philosopher's ethical views are generally reflected in an ethical *system*. An ethical system is likely to consist of a relatively small number of basic principles which are not derived, within that system, from any others. Now it is not a matter of dispute between the two metaethical schools that other general moral principles and particular moral judgments can be in some sense (to be specified below) derived from such basic principles, and that these are valid *within the system* simply in the sense that they are derivable from other statements of the system. Given that equality of rights is basically and generally desirable, then it may be inferred that any kind of racial discrimination is wrong, that segregated schools are wrong, that this particular school ought to admit Negroes, and that this particular child ought not to be excluded because of his color.

We can thus distinguish between the basic principles of a given ethical system and those other general principles and particular judgments which are directly or indirectly derivable from the former. However, the analogy with axioms and theorems of a strictly deductive system like Euclidean geometry is only a loose one because moral "axioms" must usually be supplemented by descriptive statements to yield ethical "theorems." In most cases, an 'ought' statement cannot be derived from another 'ought' statement alone but only from the former together with another, factual, premise. The latter is often too obvious to require explicit mentioning, as in the last example where we need not spell out that this child is a Negro. But it is often necessary to specify the descriptive premise. That schools ought not to be segregated follows from the principle that there ought to be no racial discrimination only if "separate but equal facilities" are in fact discriminatory, an assumption which has been disputed. Thus, given the basic ethical principle of equal rights and given certain facts, the ethical principles of racial equality and of integrated schools are demonstrably valid. The same principles would be demonstrably nonvalid with respect to an ethical system based on inequality of rights. A noncognitivist does not deny the following statement of the cognitivist philosopher St. Thomas Aquinas: "That *one must not kill* may be derived as a conclusion from the principle that *one should do harm to no man*" (*S.T.*, I–II, Q.95, A.2) and—we should add—from the (rather obvious) further premise that killing constitutes harming.

Sometimes it is the normative premise which is implied and the factual premise which is explicitly stated. By appealing to matters of fact, it is then possible to give "good reasons" for our moral choices and principles. For example, the fact that equal but separate facilities are discriminatory (assuming now that this is so) is a good reason for the moral judgment that it is wrong to have separate schools for whites and Negroes. Some cognitivists of the naturalistic school claim that in such a case the moral judgment (e.g., that separate schools are wrong) is derived from a factual judgment (e.g., that separate schools are discriminatory). Noncognitivists insist that a moral principle cannot be derived from a factual statement alone (just as it cannot be derived from another moral principle alone) but only from the former together with another, normative, premise. In our example, a noncognitivist would argue that the principle: 'separate schools are wrong' is entailed by: 'separate schools are discriminatory' *and:* 'discrimination is wrong'. Noncognitivists do not deny, however, that, *if* discrimination is wrong, then there are good reasons for integrated schools, and this policy can be rationally justified—just as maintaining separate school facilities can be shown to be rational with respect to the principle that discrimination is morally right. It may, or it may not, be possible to give "good reasons" for the wrongness—or rightness—of discrimination itself, depending on the acceptance of a still more general ethical principle.

A system of ethics is thus more like a legal than a logical system. A legal inference (e.g., that a certain law is constitutional or that the accused committed the crime) also involves references to factual considerations as well as to more general legal rules (e.g., the Constitution or the penal code).

There is an important *logical* feature which all moral judgments have in common, namely, that they are *universalizable*. Cognitivists and noncognitivists tend to agree that "the meaning of the word 'ought' and other moral words is such that a person who uses them commits himself thereby to a universal rule." (Hare, 1963, p. 30) If A says that *a* is good or right, he implicitly states that anything which is relevantly similar to *a* is also good or right. A moral or valuational judgment "logically commits the speaker to making a similar judgment about anything which is either exactly like the subject of the original judgment or like it in the relevant respects." (*Ibid.*, p. 139) We shall see later that noncognitivists criticize certain intuitionists not for relying on this principle of universalizability of ethical judgments but for drawing certain cognitivist conclusions from it.

C / BASIC ETHICAL PRINCIPLES

Cognitivists and noncognitivists are then in agreement on the following points: Judgments of rationality in general, and extrinsic value judgments in particular, are either true or false—at least in principle. Even among the intrinsic valuational and normative principles of any given ethical system, some are *demonstrably valid* within that system provided certain factual assumptions are true. These comprise all particular ethical judgments within the given system and may include a great number of general statements. This leaves only the basic principles of the system. Even here, cognitivists agree with noncognitivists in one respect, namely, that these principles cannot be validated within the given system itself. They take opposing views on only one point—but a crucial one. Cognitivists maintain that the basic principles can be shown to be true or false by considerations which fall outside the given ethical system, whereas noncognitivists deny that they can be shown to be either true or false at all.

Suppose, for example, that A advocates birth control and B opposes it. A points out the chain of necessary conditions: contraception–decrease of population–increase of the average living standard in previously overpopulated areas–general well-being. A justifies birth control policies in terms of their utility, his basic principle of political ethics. B does not challenge any of A's factual statements. He concedes that failure to check the threatened population explosion will with practical certainty lead to the greatest unhappiness of the greatest number. He realizes the ineffectiveness of the rhythm method and the futility of preaching continence. He nevertheless opposes birth control, and his only reason is that he subscribes to the ethical axiom that human life, whether actual or potential, should not be taken under any circumstances and that this goal must be given preference over that of the welfare of those actually living, now and in the future. If A and B are both noncognitivists, they will have to agree to disagree on this issue. Each will regard his own basic principle and that of his opponent to be a matter of personal commitment. Each may try to change the other's *attitude*, but not by appeal to rational argument since they admit of no disagreement about the facts. If, on the other hand, either A or B is a cognitivist, he must be convinced that he can demonstrate the truth of his own basic ethical principle and the falsity of that of his opponent. It may also be that both A and B are cognitivists. A may claim, e.g., that the principle of utility can be established by the empirical method, and B may hold that his own fundamental principle can be shown to be true as a divine enactment. If A and B are both cognitivists, and if cognitivism is the correct metaethical theory, then either *A*'s moral principle is true and *B*'s false, or vice versa; and whoever holds the incorrect ethical view is bound to abandon it, provided, of course, he is open to rational argument on the metaethical level.

I have already given some examples of conflicting basic principles of political ethics (Chap. 1, II, d). Which of two conflicting basic principles should be adopted is a matter of disagreement among political *moralists*. Whether one or the other of such conflicting principles can be shown to be true or whether adopting either constitutes a subjective moral commitment is a matter of disagreement among political *philosophers*. The answer each philosopher makes to this question will determine into which of the metaethical schools he should be classified.

II *The Natural Law Thesis and Its Denial*

The distinctions between political science, political ethics, and analytic political philosophy on the one hand and between cognitivist and noncognitivist metaethical theories on the other will prove indispensable to an understanding of the philosophy of natural law. Proponents of this philosophy, and their opponents as well, have often been unfamiliar with these categories, a fact that may account for the confusion as to the meaning of the very thesis being defended or attacked. As we shall see, the philosophy of natural law is an application of value-cognitivism to principles of political ethics of a particular, namely legal, kind. It is, then, a subcategory of cognitivism, like intuitionism and naturalism, but it is not on the same level as these two theories. Proponents of the natural law thesis do not propose a way of establishing certain principles of political or legal ethics that differs from intuitionism or naturalism, but may themselves adopt either of these two methods.

I shall disregard the numerous variations of this ancient theme, and the periodic revivals of this old doctrine, and concentrate instead on its common core. Here I shall only explicate its meaning; later chapters will deal with its critical evaluation.

1 / The Concept of Natural Law

The words 'law' and 'right' (in the sense of having a right) function in several distinct meanings. This is another source of confusion surrounding the concepts of natural law and natural rights.

a / POSITIVE LAW

'Law' in the legal sense designates a legal rule or a system of legal rules. One speaks of positive law precisely to distinguish it from the natural law. John Austin (*Jurisprudence*, Lecture 1) has given a characterization which has by now become classical: A positive law ("law properly so called") is a general* normative principle ("command"), provided with definite threats of punishment ("sanctions"), enacted by officials wielding authority (the "sovereign"), generally enforced and —for this and other reasons—generally obeyed ("habit of obedience") by those to whom the law is applicable ("the bulk of the given society"). This definition has been justly criticized because there are many kinds of legal rules which it does not cover.† However, legal

---

* It is "general in two ways; it indicates a general type of conduct and applies to a general class of persons." (Hart, p. 21)

† For example: Statutes which are binding on those who enact them are not commands given to *others* (this is true even of penal laws, at least in a constitutional democracy). Laws which confer legal powers, e.g., to make contracts or wills, are not commands. Rules of customary law are not explicitly enacted. Constitutional provisions are not commands but limitations of the legislator's powers. International law often lacks all of Austin's characteristics. (All these points are made most cogently by Hart.) Incidentally, even the law making larceny punishable, if it is a "command" at all, is addressed not to citizens but to judges and law enforcement agencies.

theorists have not yet agreed on an all-inclusive definition, and Austin's may be adequate for our purposes since it does characterize such laws as criminal statutes which most would consider the prototype of legal rules.

What is, and what is not, a law of a specified legal system is an empirical question. Thus, 'larceny is punishable by imprisonment' is a law of the legal system *S* if *S* does contain that rule, and if the rule is generally considered binding. Similarly, 'slavery is illegal in the United States' is a factual assertion to the effect that the American Constitution contains a binding rule prohibiting slavery (Thirteenth Amendment). To say that Americans have the legal right of *habeas corpus* is to refer to a provision of the American Constitution (Section IX), from which it follows that everyone, including officials, has the legal duty not to hinder anyone in the exercise of this right.

b / MORAL LAW

The words 'law' and 'right' are also used to refer to moral laws and moral rights. A moral law is the same as a moral or ethical principle. Ethical principles may be stated by anyone, not just by government officials in their official capacity; they may be addressed to anyone, including legislators and framers of constitutions; they are not normally provided with sanctions and, hence, are not enforceable; they may or may not be generally obeyed.

Here again, grammar is a treacherous guide to meaning. 'It is illegal to commit larceny' is a factual assertion to the effect that a given legal system includes a legal rule making larceny a punishable offense. 'Larceny is considered criminal, and immoral as well' is another descriptive statement. But, 'it is immoral to commit larceny' is, in spite of its indicative form, a normative statement expressing the moral judgment that one ought not to steal.

Statements about rights tend to be even more ambiguous. Take the sentence: 'American Negroes have a right to vote'. This may mean that Negroes have a *legal* right to vote, since the Constitution stipulates that "the right of citizens of the United States to vote shall not be denied . . . on account of race." (Fifteenth Amendment) Or it may mean that Negroes have the *moral* right not to be prevented from exercising this legal right, and that public authorities *should*, therefore, remove the obstacles which, in fact, exist.

The framers of the Declaration of Independence did not mean to make the—obviously false—assertion that all men do, in fact, have the legal rights of "life, liberty, and the pursuit of happiness." Nor does this document constitute an act of legislation bestowing such legal rights. It is a declaration of the *moral* principle that all men are endowed with these *moral* rights. This is not a factual assertion, like saying that all men are endowed with ears. To have a moral right to something means that others have the moral duty to act in certain ways. That men are endowed with, or have, these moral rights implies that governments have the moral duty "to secure these rights" by appropriate legislation. The same is true of the United Nations Universal Declaration of Human Rights. Its article 3, "everyone has the right to life, liberty and security of person," refers to moral rights and implicitly imposes on legislators the moral obligation to translate them into legal rights.

Law and ethics overlap. The legal injunction to drive on the right-hand side of the road has no counterpart in ethics. The ethical principle that citizens who have the franchise ought to exercise it has no counterpart in positive law (except where voting is compulsory, as it is in Belgium). However, many injunctions and prohibitions are included in legal as well as in ethical systems. Penal codes usually make only those actions criminal offenses which are prohibited by the moral code generally adopted in a society.

Like 'freedom' or 'democracy', 'law' and 'rights' have

laudatory connotations: hence the tendency to so define them in a persuasive way that they apply only to those legal rules which are deemed morally right. To give only one example: Cicero stated

that in the very definition of the term 'law' there inheres the idea and principle of choosing what is just and true. . . . What of the many deadly, the many pestilential statutes which nations put in force? These no more deserve to be called laws than the rules a band of robbers might pass in their assembly. (*Laws*, II, v)

Cicero's denial that discriminatory legal rules constitute laws is not meant to deny that such rules have been enacted and are legally valid but to affirm that they are morally wrong and ought to be abolished. But a German court decided (on February 28, 1955) that the anti-Jewish laws of 1935

were and are by reason of their unjust content and their violation of the basic demands of any legal order null and void; this law could not, even during the time of the Nazi regime, produce any *legitimate legal effect*. (Cited by Rommen, pp. 14–15)

Yet, these laws did have legally valid effects. Courts of law cannot retroactively undo such legal and political realities; they can merely declare them *morally* illegitimate and legally null and void in the future (and even this they can do only if they are empowered to exercise such legislative functions). To quote Austin again: "The existence of law is one thing; its merit or demerit is another." (*Jurisprudence*, Lecture V)

c / DESCRIPTIVE LAW

Unfortunately, the same word 'law' functions in yet a third sense: descriptive laws. I say unfortunately because this terminology further increases the tendency of confusing prescriptive laws in either the legal or the moral sense, descriptive laws of nature, and the "natural law."

Legal rules, moral principles, and descriptive laws have one linguistic feature in common: all are or can be expressed by statements which are universal (i.e., they include words such as 'all', 'any', 'whenever') and conditional ('if-then'). Examples: Larceny is punishable by imprisonment; i.e., if anyone commits larceny, he is to be punished by imprisonment. Larceny is wrong; i.e., whoever steals, does wrong. Water boils at 100° C.; i.e., whenever water is heated to 100° C., it will boil. In every free-market economy, if supply increases, cost declines.

But here the similarities end. Descriptive laws are *assertions* about regularities in nature and society. They help to *explain* what has occurred and to *predict* what will happen; they do not *prescribe* what ought to be done or avoided. Laws of nature are discovered, not enacted like positive laws or propounded like moral principles. They may be confirmed or disconfirmed but cannot be obeyed or disobeyed. To determine whether a descriptive law is true it has to be tested by reference to empirical evidence, whereas a legal rule is valid within a given legal system if it accords with other rules of the system such as the constitution or rules of competence. The question of the validity of moral norms is a controversial one, as we know, and is answered in different ways by different metaethical theories.

Descriptive laws may pertain to anything in "nature," inanimate or animate, including human behavior in general and legal actions or ethical beliefs in particular: 70 per cent of all larcenies are punished; i.e., whoever commits larceny risks a 70-per cent probability of being punished. In all societies which have the institution of private property, larceny is made a criminal offense and is considered morally wrong. Legal and moral norms, on the other hand, can be meaningfully applied only to human actions and only in situations in which actors have the choice between compliance or disobedience. Whoever enacts a legal rule or propounds an ethical principle assumes that there is no descriptive law to the effect that compliance is either impossible or unavoidable. Larceny may be made illegal or considered immoral, not so jumping over the moon or breathing.

Failure to make these distinctions goes back to scholastic philosophy which considered the physical, legal, and moral order a reflection of the will of an anthropomorphic God. In the following statements by Aquinas, 'law' has all of the three meanings at once:

the whole community of the universe is governed by the divine reason. Therefore the very notion of the government of things in God, the ruler of the universe, has the nature of a law. (S. T., I–II, Q.91, A.1)

Law is a rule and measure of acts, whereby man is induced to act or is restrained from acting; . . . . In this way, law is in all those things that are inclined to something because of some law; so that any inclination arising from a law may be called a law. (Q.90, A.1)

God "rules" all "things," including men, by enacting laws of nature, moral laws, and positive laws—the latter through His appointed rulers. He both orders and "induces" everything to conform to His laws and—which is the same—to its own "natural inclination." God "governs" the planets, and they "obey" His laws of planetary motion, just as He commands men to obey His moral law and the positive law of their divinely appointed sovereigns. There is only this difference: God has given man "free will" to disregard his own "natural inclination" and His decrees. The beginning of Montesquieu's *Spirit of the Laws* may be taken as one further example of this ambiguous usage of the term:

Laws, in the widest possible connotation, are any necessary relations arising from a thing's nature. In this sense all beings have their laws: the Deity His laws, the material world its laws, the intelligences superior to man their laws, the beasts their laws, man his laws. (I, i)

d / NATURAL LAW

Let us now take as a typical statement of natural law Locke's assertion that the

> law of nature . . . obliges everyone; and reason, which is that law, teaches all mankind who will but consult it, that . . . no one ought to harm another in his life, health, liberty, or possessions. (*Civil Government*, 6)

Locke does not mean to affirm that such acts are, in fact, illegal, let alone punishable, in some or every system of positive law, just as the Declaration of Independence does not *assert* that men everywhere have the legal right to "life, liberty, and the pursuit of happiness." That one ought to respect another's life is to Locke a *moral* duty, just as the right to life in the Declaration of Independence is a moral right. But neither Locke nor the Declaration of Independence merely propounds these ethical principles. Both say something *about* them, namely, that they constitute a law of nature or a self-evident truth. A law of nature in the descriptive sense?—No, "reason teaches" that the moral principle: 'no one ought to harm another' is true, just as the norm: 'men have certain unalienable rights' is a "self-evident truth."*

The natural law thesis does not affirm the existence of some rule of positive law, nor does it make some descriptive generalization about legal rules. The natural law thesis deals with certain *moral* rules addressed primarily to legislators. But it does not simply stipulate

* There is a difference, in this respect, between the Universal Declaration of Human Rights and the Declaration of Independence, if the latter is taken as a whole. The former merely proclaims the ethical principle that everyone has a moral right to life, liberty, and security. The latter declares that *it is self-evident* that everyone has such moral rights, and thereby expresses a metaethical view absent in the former.

what kind of positive legal rules legislators ought to
enact; it is concerned with the logical status of these
principles of legislation; it claims that they are objectively true; it is a metaethical theory. Granted, natural
law theorists may at first be concerned primarily or even
exclusively with the *advocacy* of some principle of legal
ethics, e.g., the respect for life, and only afterward attempt to *justify* their normative principle by an appeal
to natural law. However, the affirmation of the natural
law thesis itself, i.e., of the existence of natural law
principles, belongs neither to political science nor to political ethics but to analytic political philosophy.

Some other statements by proponents of the natural
law thesis will bear out this analysis.

True law is right reason in agreement with nature; it is of
universal application, unchanging and everlasting. (Cicero,
Republic, III, xxii)

The light of natural reason, whereby we discern what is
good and what is evil, which is the function of the natural
law . . . . (Aquinas, *S.T.*, I–II, Q.91, A.2)

The law of nature is a dictate of right reason, which points
out that an act, according as it is or is not in conformity
with rational nature, has in it a quality of moral baseness or
moral necessity. (Grotius, *De Jure Belli ac Pacis*, I, i, 10)

We are all born in subjection,—all born equally, high and
low, governors and governed, in subjection to one great,
immutable, pre-existent law, prior to all our devices and
prior to all our contrivances, paramount to all our ideas and
all our sensations, antecedent to our very existence, by
which we are knit and connected in the eternal frame of
the universe, out of which we cannot stir. (Burke, *Hastings*)

There is . . . an order or a disposition which human reason can discover and according to which the human will
must act in order to attune itself to the essential and necessary ends of the human being. The unwritten law, or natural law, is nothing more than that. (Maritain, 1951, p. 86)

They are the laws of a rational order of human society—in the sense that all men, when they are sincerely and lucidly rational, will regard them as self-evident. . . . When we speak of these principles as natural laws, we must be careful. They are not scientific "laws" like the laws of the motions of the heavenly bodies. They do not describe human behavior as it is. They prescribe what it should be. (Lippmann, pp. 95–96)

This, then, is the common core of the various natural law theories. There are certain principles of political ethics which are objectively true. They stipulate what kind of positive laws should be enacted, enforced, and obeyed. These make up the natural law. They are "eternal and unchangeable . . . valid for all nations and all times." (Cicero, *Republic*, III, xxii) Consequently every legislator has the moral duty to legislate in conformity to them. "Thus the law of nature stands as an eternal rule to all men, legislators as well as others." (Locke, *Civil Government*, 135) Positive law in agreement with natural law is objectively just. Positive law in conflict with natural law constitutes "unjust law," morally wrong though legally valid.* The validity of the natural law itself is not affected by a legislator's ignorance of its precepts or by his disagreement with its norms or by his failure to translate them into positive law.

Natural law is always conceived of as a small number of general and basic principles of political and legal morality, such as the protection of human life or the keeping of contractual promises. We have seen that the "theorems" of an ethical system cannot usually be logi-

---

* Cicero continues (*loc. cit.*): "It is a sin to try to alter this law, nor is it allowable to attempt to repeal any part of it, and it is impossible to abolish it entirely." If it is *impossible* to annul the natural law, how can it be morally *wrong* to do so? Evidently Cicero meant that it is impossible to do anything about its *cognitive* validity, even though it is possible (though not permissible) to restrict its *legal* validity through legislation which is incompatible with its principles.

cally derived from its "axioms" without reference to further, factual, premises. The adaptation of positive to natural law requires, therefore, legislative latitude and skill. We shall see later that Aquinas characterizes the relationship between positive and natural law as one of "determination" requiring "human reason," but not in the sense of mere deductive reasoning.

Natural law theorists are especially prone to define the concept of positive law persuasively to apply only to legal rules which are just, that is, insofar as they are in agreement with the natural law itself. To quote Aquinas again:

Every human law has just so much of the nature of law as it is derived from the law of nature. But if in any point it departs from the law of nature, it is no longer a law but a perversion of law. (*S.T.*, I–II, Q.95, A.2)

Similarly, a post-Nazi court declared (in a decision of February 8, 1952) that

the fact that the Hitler regime, as long as it was in power, was *legally competent to* posit legally valid laws and decrees . . . does not mean that all of them were—in the true meaning of the word—"Recht" if and insofar as in their *content* they violated the commands of natural law or the universally valid moral laws of Christian Western civilization. (Cited by Rommen, p. 15)

'Law' is used in 'natural law' in the sense of moral law. But 'law' also connotes that these principles are, like descriptive laws, discovered and not, like positive laws, enacted, that they simultaneously describe and prescribe, and that they may be about anything in the "universe."

Law is not a product of human thought, nor is it any enactment of peoples, but something eternal which rules the whole universe by its wisdom in command and prohibition. (Cicero, *Laws*, II, 14)

The word 'natural' conveys the same idea; it also indicates that such norms are discovered by our "natural faculties" or by "natural reason," and that they are part of the "natural order of things." "A rule of justice is natural that has the same validity everywhere, and does not depend on our accepting it or not." (Aristotle, *Ethics*, 1134b)

The thesis that the moral norm: 'no one ought to take another's life' is a principle of natural law means then roughly the same as that the moral rule: 'no one ought to take another's life' is objectively true, and that legislators have then the moral duty to translate this ethical principle into positive law by making murder a punishable offense. A similar interpretation applies to the concept of natural rights. Take the French Declaration of 1789: "The aim of every political association is the preservation of the natural and imprescriptible rights of man. These rights are liberty, property, security, and resistance to oppression." That liberty is a natural rather than a legal or merely moral right is again a metaethical statement. It affirms that the statement: 'man has a moral right to liberty' is objectively true, and that, therefore, any political association ought to aim at its preservation.

To deny the natural law thesis is to hold the following view: There are no objective standards to guide legislators or citizens. Committing murder may be deemed morally wrong, and the law making murder punishable may be considered right. However, the categories of truth and falsity are not applicable to such moral judgments unless they are derived from other, more basic, principles. There are no objective grounds that could serve to establish the truth or falsity of basic principles of politics and legislation.

2 / Natural Law and Political Ethics

Since the natural law thesis is a theory of political philosophy, it is misleading to contrast it with the social contract theory or the organic theory of the state, as is often done. These are descriptive hypotheses about the origin and nature of political systems. They are theories of political science, not of political metaethics (and not of political ethics either, although they have important normative implications). It is true that natural law theorists such as Aquinas did not consider political society to be based on the social contract. Conversely, Hobbes, one of the foremost exponents of the social contract theory, denied the natural law thesis (even though he used natural law terminology, as we shall see). On the other hand, Locke adhered both to the political *philosophy* of natural law and to the political *theory* of the social contract. Similarly, Rousseau's work contains many references to natural law, and also comes at least close to viewing the state as an organic whole.

Another current misconception is to oppose the *metaethical* theory of natural law to utilitarianism, the *ethical* theory which makes the moral worth of actions (and of political institutions) dependent on their contributions to human happiness. It so happens that certain utilitarians, and especially Bentham, have criticized the natural law thesis. But it is perfectly consistent to maintain that the principle of utility is itself a principle of natural law. Austin held this view explicitly, if we interpret his use of "Divine law" in the sense of natural law:

An act which is generally useful, conforms to the Divine law as known through the principle of utility. . . . An act which were generally useful, the Divine law, as known through the principle of utility, has conferred on the sovereign government a right to do. (*Jurisprudence*, Lecture VI)

Just as with cognitivism generally, the natural law doctrine has, as a matter of historical fact, been invoked to justify various, and often conflicting, doctrines of political ethics. The Catholic Church has stressed, ever since medieval times, that "the natural law enjoins obedience to regularly constituted authority" ("Ethics," *Catholic Encyclopedia*, Vol. V, p. 562) and that obedience to positive law is, therefore, a natural obligation, however "unjust" it may be and however "tyrannical" the ruler, for "he who resists the authorities resists what God has appointed" (Rom. 13:1–2); the only exception being laws which enjoin disobedience to God's commands. On the other hand, natural law theory of the post-Reformation period, especially in its secularized version, has emphasized that the people's right to disobey, resist, and rebel against any government which fails to protect their natural rights is itself a natural right. Thus, the Declaration of Independence lists among the "self-evident truths" that "it is the Right of the People to alter or to abolish" a government not merely if it should enjoin disobedience to some divine command but "whenever any Form of Government becomes destructive of these Ends"; i.e., when it fails to secure men's basic rights.

Freedom of thought and speech has been held to be both commanded and prohibited by natural law. The French Declaration of 1789 states that "the free communication of ideas and of opinions is one of the most precious of the rights of man"; i.e., of the natural rights of man and citizen. But the Papal Encyclical *Immortale Dei* (1885) declared that "the unrestrained freedom of thinking and of openly making known one's thoughts is not inherent in the rights of citizens," but that such "tenets of unbridled licence" are, on the contrary, "at variance on many points with not only the Christian, but even the natural law." Similarly, slavery and other forms of inequality have been perpetrated in the name of natural law, the same philosophy which has also emphasized the equality of man's natural rights. On the other hand, one and the same political doctrine—that of equal basic rights—has been defended both by those who consider these rights to be natural rights and by others who deny the natural law philosophy.

The fact that natural law has served as a foundation of conservative as well as of progressive and even revolutionary doctrines is no valid argument against the natural law thesis itself. Logically, any metaethical theory is compatible with any ethical theory. However, those who regard, say, freedom of thought as a natural law principle are bound to consider a claim that natural law enjoins restricting freedom of speech as grave a mistake as the denial of the natural law thesis itself. If the natural law thesis is valid, then upholding and restricting freedom of speech cannot both be commands of natural law (it may, of course, be the case that the natural law is silent on the subject).

3 / Natural Law and Philosophy of Political Ethics

a / NATURAL LAW AND VALUE-COGNITIVISM

The natural law thesis entails value-cognitivism. Value-cognitivism holds that there are objectively true basic valuational or normative principles. This is precisely what the natural law thesis claims to be the case; it is an application of cognitivism to moral principles of politics. And whoever holds that there are such valid principles of legal and political ethics must be classified as a natural law philosopher, regardless of whether or not he uses the term 'natural law'. Plato was no doubt a proponent of the natural law theory, even though this concept was not introduced until after his time. Indeed, the future guardians of the Republic

must lift up the eye of the soul to gaze on that which sheds light on all things; and when they have seen the Good itself, take it as a pattern for the right ordering of the state and of the individual, themselves included. (*Republic*, 540)

The Declaration of Independence does not include the word 'natural', yet it is essentially a declaration of natural law and natural rights.

Anyone who appeals to natural law has then the burden of demonstrating what he regards as the content of natural law. By justifying his particular version of natural law, he would substantiate the natural law thesis in general, and value-cognitivism itself. However, proponents of natural law often do not seem to realize that they have espoused the metaethical theory of cognitivism and, hence, do not see the necessity of even raising this question, let alone of answering it. They seem satisfied to *proclaim* that "there is in fact a true law" or to *profess* their "unshakable faith in moral and legal values above and beyond the chaos and relativity of mere empirical 'giveness' " (Chroust, p. 80) or to *assume* that "doubtless, there is a universal justice emanating from reason alone." (Rousseau, *Social Contract*, II, vi) To proclaim is not to demonstrate; faith is no substitute for proof; and assumptions must be warranted. We shall be concerned only with those natural law philosophers who have advanced arguments in support of their philosophy, either of the intuitionistic or the naturalistic type.

Natural law entails cognitivism; but does cognitivism entail natural law, or can one be a cognitivist and yet deny the natural law thesis? Some natural law philosophers conceive of the norms of natural law as pertaining to the whole of morality, individual as well as social and political. Plato's statement quoted above is a case in point. Cicero states that "law is the highest reason, implanted in nature, which commands what ought to be done and forbids the opposite." (*Laws*, I, vi) Aquinas considers it "the function of natural law" to enable us to "discern what is good and what is evil."

According to this view, any principle of morality discernible as valid constitutes a principle of natural law.

However, natural law is more often, and more plausibly, conceived as encompassing not "the Good," in general, but only principles of political and legal ethics. It would be possible, and logically consistent, to hold that there are objectively ascertainable standards of individual morality or of aesthetic beauty (or at least of ugliness!) but not of political right and wrong. There have also been cognitivists in the political sphere who have denied the natural law thesis. We shall see later that Bentham regarded utility as a demonstrably valid "principle of morals and legislation"; yet, he did not consider it a principle of natural law, perhaps because he regarded it as too general to be directly translatable into positive legal rules. However, Bentham criticized explicitly only the doctrine of natural rights, denying that one could conceive of individual legal or moral rights independent of positive law and actual government. Yet, by attempting to justify the principle of utility as a basic principle of political ethics, Bentham came at least close to the very theory of natural law he implicitly criticized in attacking the doctrine of natural rights.

b / VALUE-NONCOGNITIVISM AND THE DENIAL OF NATURAL LAW

Since proponents of the natural law thesis are necessarily cognitivists, it follows that the denial of cognitivism implies the denial of the natural law thesis. Indeed, if *any* basic ethical principle is a matter of subjective commitment, then basic ethical principles as to what kind of legal rules should be enacted and obeyed have no cognitive status either.

Here again it is easy to be misled by terminology. Just as there are cognitivists who belong to the natural law school without using the expression 'natural law', there are noncognitivists who do use this expression even though they must, as noncognitivists, disagree with the natural law thesis. Both Hobbes and Hume are cases in point, as we shall see in greater detail later.

Noncognitivism implies the denial of natural law; but does the denial of natural law entail noncognitivism? We have seen that it is possible, theoretically, to hold that basic norms of political ethics are a matter of subjective commitment but that there are objectively valid valuational or normative judgments in other areas. For our purposes, we may disregard these distinctions. In turning next to a critical examination of the various types of philosophies of political ethics, the natural law controversy will not be considered separately but in the larger context of the cognitivist-noncognitivist debate.

3

Intuitionism as a Political Philosophy

I shall now turn to a critical examination of various political philosophies in the light of the metaethical categories of intuitionism, naturalism, and noncognitivism. I am well aware of the difficulty of applying these modern categories to *ethical* thinkers of the past. It is even more difficult to apply them to *political* thinkers, not only of the past but even of the present, because most political theorists do not think in such terms. To place a system of political ethics into this metaethical scheme usually requires interpretation, which in turn involves the danger of misinterpretation, of trying to fit the system into what might in some cases turn out to be a Procrustean bed. To be aware of this danger is at least a necessary condition for avoiding it. In any case, the attempt seems to me well worthwhile because I consider these metaethical concepts excellent tools for arriving at an analytic understanding, a critical evaluation, and a comparative view of different systems of political philosophy.

In the present chapter I shall examine intuitionistic political philosophies, those which hold that basic principles of political ethics can be known to be true through moral or religious or rational insight.

I *Based on Moral Insight*

1 / Plato

Among philosophers concerned with politics, Plato may well be considered the most outspoken of those who regard intuition as the source of *all* knowledge, including the knowledge of goodness in general and the knowledge of justice in the state. Plato contrasts the world of concrete and visible phenomena with the world of abstract and invisible forms or ideas or essences. The former is made up of the multiplicity of ever-changing objects, of chairs and fires, of things which are equal or unequal, of art works which are beautiful or ugly, of actions which are just or unjust. The latter is characterized by oneness and immutability: one form of chairness, one essence of fire, one idea of mathematical equality, one form of beauty and justice.

Sense experience apprehends only the appearance of things. It is the source of mere "opinion"—subjective, uncertain, and deceptive. It provides only images of reality—the shadows of the allegory of the cave—but does not unveil reality itself. Trusting our senses is an obstacle to authentic knowledge. When the soul

looks towards that twilight world of things that come into existence and pass away, its sight is dim and it has only opinions and beliefs which shift to and fro, and now it seems like a thing that has no intelligence. (*Republic*, 508)

True knowledge is knowledge of reality behind appearances, knowledge of the single forms behind the multiple objects: "The perfectly real is perfectly knowable, and the utterly unreal is entirely unknowable." (476)

Further, the many things, we say, can be seen, but are not objects of rational thought; whereas the Forms are objects of thought, but invisible. (507)

It is only when we have grasped the idea of equality that we can judge whether two objects are equal. Without the perception of goodness or beauty or justice we are unable to judge whether a thing is good; a work of art beautiful, an action just.

So when people have an eye for the multitude of beautiful things or of just actions or whatever it may be, but can neither behold Beauty or Justice itself nor follow a guide who would lead them to it, we shall say that all they have is beliefs, without any real knowledge of the objects of their belief. . . . But what of those who contemplate the realities themselves as they are for ever in the same unchanging state? Shall we not say that they have, not mere belief, but knowledge? (479)

It is "through the discourse of reason unaided by any of the senses" that one is to gain knowledge of the forms. (532) And by 'reason' Plato can mean in this context only direct intuitive insight. He does not actually use the term 'intuition' but speaks of the ability to perceive, apprehend, contemplate, grasp, gaze upon, and even see the forms, invisible as they are. He evidently uses these expressions not in their usual meaning of sense perception but in the figurative sense of intuitive insight.

Ethics is the highest form of cognition, and political ethics its most important part. "In the world of knowledge, the last thing to be perceived and only with great difficulty is the essential Form of Goodness." (517) Knowledge of the Good is both a necessary and a sufficient condition for acting wisely and justly. "Without having had a vision of this Form no one can act with wisdom." (517) Conversely, who knows the Good will act morally. Those who "have seen the Good itself, [will] take it as a pattern for the right ordering of the state and of the individual, themselves included." (540) There are, then, certain moral principles which are objectively true and can be known as such on the basis of correct intuitive moral insight. This faculty is available only to a small minority, and to them only after arduous training.

Of the great political philosophers, Plato was one of the few who were as much interested in metaethical as in ethical issues. In the *Republic* he was more concerned with emphasizing that political justice can be known than with specifying its content. The ideal commonwealth should aim "not to make any one class specially happy" nor even to make all citizens as happy as possible—this would be a happiness "like that of a party of peasants feasting at a fair"—"but to secure the greatest possible happiness for the community as a whole" and to allow the several classes only "such measure of happiness as their nature will compass." (420–421) The ideal commonwealth is, then, a rigidly stratified society.

When each order—tradesman, Auxiliary, Guardian—keeps to its own proper business in the commonwealth and does its own work, that is justice and what makes a just society. (434)

Accordingly, absolute political authority should be placed in the hands of those "who are naturally fitted to combine philosophic study with political leadership" (474), i.e., of the philosopher-kings who alone are capable of acceding to the vision of the Good.

How the future rulers are to be educated and selected is spelled out in detail in the *Republic*, but that does not concern us here. Nor is it our task to deal critically with Plato's theory of ideas. We are concerned with one crucial question: Can the political system which Plato advocates be justified by the argument that moral insight reveals its rightness? Are there any propositions which have to be accepted as true because they have been intuited by someone to be true? Let us look at three cases.

1 A states that this rose is red and B says that it is yellow. Obviously, this matter can be settled in an objective way, because the statement under dispute can be tested by reference to observational evidence which is, at least in principle, available to anyone. If the rose turns out to be red, B will—unless he is subject to excessive pride—acknowledge that he was mistaken in this instance or that he is color-blind.

2 A states that he "knows it in his bones" that a certain candidate will win the next election, and B claims that he knows "intuitively" that that candidate will lose. If he wins, we conclude that A's insight turned out to be true, and B himself is likely to admit that he had a pseudo-intuition. But is A's statement justified *because* of his insight? No, because "after the facts are in" this statement too is confirmed by publicly available evidence. There is no denial that we sometimes experience a "flash of intuition"; e.g., when we suddenly have the conviction that something is the case or will happen, or the feeling that we "understand" a mathematical proof or "see" a causal connection. Here, the word 'intuition' refers to a psychological phenomenon; it describes (but hardly explains) how we are sometimes led to make some assertion—which may be true or false. Whether it *is* true or false depends on certain objective logical or empirical criteria which are quite independent of our subjective feeling of certitude.

3 A claims that his vision of the essential nature of the Good has revealed to him that the Platonic type of ideal commonwealth is the best. B asserts that moral

insight discloses utilitarianism as the true basic principle of political ethics, and that it can, therefore, be shown that government ought to aim at the greatest possible happiness, not of the commonwealth as a whole (whatever that may mean), but of all citizens alike, regardless of class differences. If Plato's intuitionistic metaethics is correct, there must be an objective method by which anyone could decide, at least in principle, whose intuition is the valid one, that of A, the Platonist, or that of B, the utilitarian, or if neither one is. But what is the criterion? Agreement among the majority? Not according to Plato who emphasizes that true knowledge is available only to the minority of philosophically minded. If both A and B claim—as each well might—that he, and not his antagonist, belongs to this highest class, by what objective criterion are we to decide *this* question? Anyhow, to argue that something is desirable *because* it is held to be desirable by some group (whether the majority or a minority) would be taking a naturalistic position, not Plato's approach. Plato does not hold that his ideal commonwealth is good because the select few think that it is but, on the contrary, that they intuit its goodness because it *is* good. B, who would readily admit that he is color-blind or that he had a wrong intuition about the election, is unlikely to concede that he is "value-blind." But neither will A concede that *his* "knowledge of the Good" constitutes a mere "opinion." I do not believe that Plato has provided an objective criterion for the truth of insights into the goodness of things in general and of political institutions in particular. I conclude, therefore, that Platonic insight, far from leading to objective ethical knowledge, is merely another name for anyone's subjective moral commitments.

2 / Jean-Jacques Rousseau

Unlike Plato, Rousseau constructed neither a general philosophical system nor a systematic philosophy of political ethics. Implicitly, however, his political writings are based on the Platonic assumption that political justice can be known through correct moral insight. Like Plato, Rousseau searches for *true* principles of the good society. This is indicated by the first sentence of the *Social Contract*: "I mean to inquire if, in the civil order, there can be any sure and legitimate rule of administration"; in other words, whether there are constitutional principles (that is what Rousseau means by "rule of administration") which can be known with *certainty* ("sure") to be *morally* legitimate. We find in Rousseau's writings scattered, but important, references to the natural law thesis. For example:

What is well and in conformity with order is so by the nature of things and independently of human conventions. . . . Doubtless, there is a universal justice emanating from reason alone. (*Social Contract*, II, vi)

It is not more permissible to infringe upon the natural laws through the social contract than it is permissible to infringe upon the positive laws through private contracts. (*Letters from the Mountain*, Letter VI)

What is the source of man's knowledge of the principles of universal justice, i.e., of natural law? "The eternal laws of nature . . . are written in the depths of his heart by conscience and reason." (*Emile*, V) Even though Rousseau uses the term 'reason', the emphasis is on the heart, the seat of "natural feeling."

It is then certain that compassion is a natural feeling, ... In a word, it is rather in this natural feeling than in any subtle arguments that we must look for the cause of that repugnance, which every man would experience in doing evil, even independently of the maxims of education. (*Inequality*)

Taken in connection with the previous statement from *Emile*, this passage may well be interpreted in the sense that "natural feeling" leads men to know as well as to do what is objectively right, although Rousseau does not say so explicitly. Man's natural instinct has been obscured by the artificial contraptions of civilization. He cannot return to his original state of innocence; yet he can attain the knowledge of justice by uniting with his fellow citizens into a political community directed by the "general will."

Rousseau's general will is not the sum of the preferences of each citizen, but "the will . . . of the body of the people." (*Social Contract*, II, ii)

The body politic, therefore, is also a moral being possessed of a will; and this general will, which tends always to the preservation and welfare of the whole and of every part, and is the source of the laws, constitutes for all the members of the State, in their relations to one another and to it, the rule of what is just or unjust. (*Political Economy*)

Unlike Plato with his select few, Rousseau holds that justice is revealed to all—not, however, as single individuals but as members of the body politic and, hence, of the general will. "The general will is always right and tends to the public advantage." (*Social Contract*, II, iii)

This general will manifests itself in the general assembly of all citizens in a direct democracy, which Rousseau considered the ideal form of government. However, it is not the case that right is whatever this legislative assembly happens to decide. Justice is, for Rousseau no less than for Plato, an objective entity; and it so happens that the majority of the assembly, like Plato's philosopher-statesmen, tends to ascertain what is objectively just.

When in the popular assembly a law is proposed, what the people is asked is not exactly whether it approves or rejects the proposal, but whether it is in conformity with the general will, which is their will. Each man, in giving his vote, states his opinion on that point; and the general will is found by counting votes. When therefore the opinion that is contrary to my own prevails, this proves neither more nor less than that I was mistaken, and that what I thought to be the general will was not so. (*Social Contract*, IV, ii)

Since it is evident that "the most general will is always the most just also, and that the voice of the people is in fact the voice of God" (*Political Economy*), sovereignty is located in the general will, and government is merely its executive. For the same reason, "the sovereign power need give no guarantee to its subjects, because it is impossible for the body to wish to hurt all its members." (*Social Contract*, I, vii) Unlike Locke and like Plato, Rousseau denies that citizens have any natural rights against the sovereign.

On the whole, however, Rousseau's political ethics, with its emphasis on popular sovereignty and on equality of political and legal rights as well as duties, is at the opposite pole from Plato's. We have here a good illustration of two opposite systems of political ethics with a similar—in this case, intuitionistic—metaethical basis.

Here the same question arises again. How does one know that Rousseau's democratic egalitarianism is objectively just and that Plato's hierarchical commonwealth is not? Because it is willed by the general will? But how do we know *what it is* that the general will wills? Where do we find the general will in the first place? In some instances, Rousseau tells us that the general will is the same as the will of the majority of the legislative assembly in a direct democracy. But Rousseau himself recognizes that direct democracy is not even a practical possibility, let alone a reality in the area of the large national state. At other places, Rousseau claims that the general will is the will of the body politic as a whole, rather than that of any number of citizens. But is there such a thing as a group will? It is not clear whether Rousseau's picture of the state as a living organism is to be taken as a mere allegory or whether he literally subscribed to the organic theory of the state. In either case, it is impossible to find an empirical referent for the concept of general will. Anyhow, Rousseau does not argue that a law is just because it has been enacted by the general will, but that "the general will tends to equality" (*Social Contract*, II, i) because egalitarian rules are objectively just. But then we are driven back to the original question: How does the general will (whatever it may be) know or how do those who compose it (whoever they may be) know what kind of positive legal rules correspond to natural justice? Rousseau has nothing to fall back on but our "natural feelings" and the "depths of our hearts." But what if these should lead you and me in opposite directions? What objective criterion is there by which to decide whose heart is in the right place?

Rousseau cannot, of course, be held responsible for the doctrines and actions of those political leaders, from Robespierre to Hitler, who claimed, in good or in bad faith, that they were merely and humbly executing the general will of their people known to them intuitively, and that they could, therefore, dispense with the artificial contraptions of representative institutions. Their views and, especially, their policies are the very denial of Rousseau's political *ethics*; but the point here is that they are not incompatible with his political *philosophy*. Rousseau's normative doctrines are of great significance, and so are his contributions to the understanding of the political process (which I did not even mention here); but his philosophical framework was built on the weak foundation of moral insight.

3 / Carl Friedrich

The metaethical theory that values and norms are objective entities which can be apprehended through moral intuition has its contemporary adherents, among political scientists as well as among philosophers. As an illustration, I shall quote some passages from Carl J. Friedrich's *Man and His Government*. As plainly as Plato and more explicitly than Rousseau, Friedrich affirms that values are discovered in objects.

The valuer's role is to discover the value, not to create or constitute it. . . . [Values] are facts in the sense of being experienced as being there. In other words, the values exist, whether there is someone to recognize them or not. . . . An act of moral goodness is good independently of any persons present to appreciate it. (pp. 62–64)

Both facts and values are a matter of experience. "The experiencing of value is as much a primary experience as observation of facts devoid of value." (p. 55) And just as the basic colors are "nearly universally experienced," so "the basic values are experienced by most persons." Hence, "the occasional occurrence of value-blind persons need not disturb us unduly." (p. 56)

Friedrich uses the term 'experience' to refer to the discovery of values as well as of facts. However, his use of the expression 'value-blind' suggests the view that values and facts are not experienced in the same way, that the latter are apprehended by our five senses and the former by a sixth, moral, sense. Any of the senses may deceive us and lead us into making mistaken judgments, whether of fact or of value. Both kinds of judgments are, nevertheless, objectively either true or false.

Experience may deceive, and often does. This patent observation applies to all kinds of experience and, therefore, does not provide a basis for contrasting value experience with other kinds of experience. That something may be believed to be valuable when it is not parallels the fact that something may be believed to be straight when it is not, such as the well-known optical illusion of a broken stick seen in a glass of water. (p. 55)

To repeat, the parallel between statements of fact and value judgments does not hold. That this rose is red and that those who deny this fact are color-blind can be established by an objective, i.e., intersubjective, procedure. Similarly, there is an operational test by which anyone can confirm the hypothesis that this submerged stick is straight: pull it out of the water and it will appear straight. On the other hand, take a situation in which the majority and the minority in a given society disagree as to what is intrinsically valuable or morally good. There is no way of deciding whether the former experienced the objective value entity and the latter was deceived by *its* value experience, or whether, on the contrary, the majority happened to be value-blind and the "deviant" value judgment based on true moral insight. It seems to me that this form of intuitionism does not provide an objective criterion by which to assess the truth of fundamental principles of ethics in general and of political ethics in particular, be it the desirability of Plato's hierarchical commonwealth or of Rousseau's egalitarian democracy or of constitutional democracy, which happens to be Friedrich's model of the good society.

II *Based on Religious Insight*

1 / St. Augustine and John Calvin

According to another variety of intuitionism, the most fundamental principles of morality have been enacted by God. But they can be known not by the mere fact that God has revealed them through the written words

of the Holy Scriptures. They can be known to be true
because those who have the true faith have a direct religious insight leading them to the knowledge of God
and, thereby, to the knowledge of His revealed moral
truths independently of the sacred texts. It is an argument from faith, not from authority.

To St. Augustine, the true faith is, of course, the
Christian faith which is the key to all understanding,
including the knowledge of good and evil.

Understanding is the reward of faith. Therefore do not
seek to understand in order to believe, but believe that thou
mayest understand; since 'except ye believe, ye shall not
understand.' [Isa. 7:9] (*In Iohannis Evangelium Tractatus*, XXIX, 6)

As distinguished from active reasoning, faith is the passive assent to God's revelation. Reason presupposes
faith, since knowledge of the truth consists in the
vision of the truth in God made possible through divine
illumination. There is a chain of necessary conditions
leading from faith to reason to knowledge to wisdom to
blessedness—the ultimate goal open only to the minority of the elect.

Knowledge of the truth includes knowledge of the
principles of morality. "Thus, just as the human mind
perceives eternal theoretic truths in the light of God, so
it perceives, in the same light, practical truths or principles which should direct the free will." (Copleston, p.
83) Like the truths of religion, those of the natural law
are transcribed by God into the human mind, "as the
impression from a ring passes into the wax, yet does not
leave the ring." (*De Trinitate*, XIV, xv, 21) The basic
precept of natural law is the golden rule, which comprises more specific social rules such as the prohibition
of murder, violence, and theft.

The hand of our Maker in our very hearts hath written this
truth, *That which to thyself thou wouldest not have done,*

do not thou to another. (Matt. vii, 12) Of this truth, even
before that the Law was given, no one was suffered to be
ignorant, in order that there might be some rule whereby
might be judged even those to whom Law had not been
given. But lest men should complain that something had
been wanting for them, there hath been written also in
tables that which in their heart they read not. (*Enarrationes in Psalmos*, LVII, 1)

Augustinean natural law is, thus, not natural in the literal sense of being part of the natural order, except that
nature itself is created by God. Natural law is essentially
supernatural, divine law. Since God is omnipotent, He
could have enacted different commands. To know
God's law, one must be attuned to the revelation of His
will. Both the content of the moral law and its truth are
derived from God's will. As the passage just quoted indicates, the divine moral law antedates the fall of Adam
as well as the written law which God has promulgated
explicitly in the Ten Commandments and the Gospels.
These explicit divine ordinances merely make the natural law more readily known, thus making it easier for
man to act accordingly. Man is bound to comply with
God's precepts, not simply because He has enacted
them explicitly but because they constitute moral truths
which man has the ability to know through the true
faith. If it is in fact almost impossible for man to gain
knowledge of good and evil, and to do good even when
he knows it, this is a consequence of his basic sinfulness.
Only the true faith can bring men back to true knowledge and right actions and will lead some—those pre-
destined to be saved—to salvation.

Augustine's view that "whatever is good is so by the
divine blessing, and whatever is bad is so by the divine
judgment" (*Contra Faustum*, XXII, 79) is echoed by
Calvin's belief that "God's will is so much the highest
rule of righteousness that whatever he wills, by the very
fact that he wills it, must be considered righteous." (*Institutes*, III, xxiii, 2) Calvin, too, holds that man can

know the will of God, and hence know what is objectively just, because He has revealed His will to him.

It is a fact that the law of God, which we call the moral law, is nothing else than a testimony of natural law, and of that conscience which God has engraved upon the minds of men. (*Institutes*, IV, xx, 16)

2 / Emil Brunner and Reinhold Niebuhr

As modern examples of Augustinean metaethics we may take the views of two contemporary Protestant theologians who have dealt with political problems, the Swiss Emil Brunner and the American Reinhold Niebuhr. Brunner's *Justice and the Social Order* deals primarily with the problem of the *knowledge* of political justice. "A knowledge of the just on a clear and firm foundation is a first, and even indispensable step towards putting justice into action." (p. 3) Brunner also takes the cognitivist position that "there is a valid criterion, a justice which stands above us all, a challenge presented *to* us, not *by* us, a standard rule of justice binding on every state and every system of law." (p. 8)

How do we know the valid criterion that determines what positive laws are just? Brunner emphatically adopts St. Augustine's view that "the idea of justice and the concept of a divine law of justice are one and the same thing," (p. 46) and that this divine law can only be known to "the believer in the God of Scriptural revelation." (p. 48) "We may doubt justice, as we may doubt truth. But one thing is impossible—to believe in justice and yet to reject the divine law of justice." (p. 46) In other words, belief in justice implies belief in the Gospels. Consequently, a non-Christian who rejects the Scriptures cannot believe in justice and, hence, cannot know the valid criteria of justice.

Again following Augustine, Brunner considers "the law of nature [to be] the eternal unwritten laws of the Creator," (p. 95) which is supernatural: "In the

Christian law of nature, nature is the divine creative ordinance of God, of the God who revealed His will to mankind in Jesus Christ." (p. 85) Brunner rejects the post-Augustinean "purely rationalistic conception" (p. 92) which holds, as we shall see in the next section, that man can know natural law by means of his reason alone, without recourse to Christian faith. Since

sin obscures the capacity of human reason even in spheres which are accessible to rational knowledge . . ., we cannot dispense with the specific divine revelation even for the comprehension of mundane justice based on the knowledge of the order of creation. (p. 91)

The natural law contains, first of all, the general principle of justice: to each his due. It is related to that of human equality, which, once again, "is not to be sought in abstract reason, nor in a general order of being, but in the will of the living God." (p. 39) Divine revelation becomes quite specific. For instance, "private property is a right established by creation." (p. 148) "In fulfillment of the Creator's gift, man is also, by divine ordinance, granted freedom to use his sexual faculties" (p. 60)—with some limitations.

Niebuhr holds similar views. He claims that there are

some general principles of justice, which define the right order of life in a community. . . . Every human society does have something like a natural-law concept; for it assumes that there are more immutable and purer principles of justice than those actually embodied in its obviously relative laws. (1944, pp. 67–68)

The final resource against idolatrous national communities, who refuse to acknowledge any law beyond their power, must be found in the recognition of universal law by individuals, who have a source of moral insight beyond the partial and particular national communities. (*Ibid.*, p. 82)

Every society needs working principles of justice, as criteria for its positive law and system of restraints. The profoundest of these actually transcend reason and lie rooted in religious conceptions of the meaning of existence. (*Ibid.*, p. 71)

The prophetic faith in a God who is both the ground and the ultimate fulfillment of existence, who is both the creator and the judge of the world, is thus involved in every moral situation. (1935, p. 105.)

There are, thus, "general principles of justice" or of natural law. They can be known through "moral insight" which, in turn, has its source in "religious ideas" and, more specifically, in the evangelical law of the Christian faith. There can be no understanding of the "profoundest" of these principles without faith, contrary to the rationalistic natural law conception of Thomism which overrates man's capacity to reason and disregards his innate sinfulness.

Niebuhr's metaethical views tend toward irrationalism in a double sense: irrational religious faith is the only way to discover objective justice. Even so, justice remains incomprehensive and inapplicable to the everyday world of politics. The law of justice is essentially the law of love: it lacks specific content and can at best be approximated by concrete political institutions and policies. In this respect Niebuhr differs from Brunner who believes that the divine law contains specific injunctions to which the political order can and ought to conform in a literal sense.

A quotation from Martin Luther King may serve as a final example of this view:

How does one determine whether a law is just or unjust? A just law is a man-made code that squares with the moral law or the law of God. An unjust law is a code that is out of harmony with the moral law. (King, p. 85)

We are not told explicitly how one can know the law of God, but we must presume that divine revelation would be the answer.

The theologians whose views we have just examined do not merely advocate that what God wills ought to be done. This would be a principle of *normative ethics* which presupposes, of course, the belief that there is a God, that God issues commands, and that, say, the golden rule is commanded by God. It does not, however, entail any view as to the truth of this general ethical principle. Even a noncognitivist could subscribe to the ethical norm that one ought to comply with God's will, whatever it may be, and however arbitrary it may seem. However, Augustine and his followers hold that, in Calvin's words, "what He wills must be considered just," and this presumably means that what God wills is objectively just and what He commands is objectively right. Calvin's statement, thus, expresses a *metaethical* thesis; namely, that the moral precepts emanating from God have an objective quality and must be followed because they are objectively right. Thus, religious faith reveals not only the existence of God and the content of His enactments but their objectivity as well. More specifically, faith enables one to *discover* the following moral principle: 'whatever God commands ought to be done; whatever God prohibits ought to be avoided'. Since faith also reveals the fact that God has prohibited murder, it follows that the prohibition against murder is an objective moral principle.

There can be no dispute that this conclusion follows logically from the two premises. But are *they* true? Even if they are, knowledge that they are true is admittedly limited to those who are endowed with true religious insight. Mere belief in an abstract Supreme Being is not enough. Knowledge of the principles of natural or moral or divine law is accessible only to the Christian "believer in the God of Scriptural revelation." It follows that agnostics and atheists cannot know which principles of justice are objectively true; they can have no knowledge of God's will since they doubt or even deny His existence. Even those who adhere to some religious faith other than the Christian are excluded from insight into these truths, as Brunner clearly implies.

Now, it is an empirical fact that the Ten Commandments and the golden rule have been held to be not only morally obligatory but also true principles of morality by non-Christians and by atheists. The only possible reply would be that they have adopted the correct ethical as well as metaethical view, but for the wrong reason. However, the argument that a moral principle is true because it was uttered by God is, indeed, not acceptable except to someone who happens to believe in an anthropomorphic God who does issue commands, if not in the God of St. Augustine and Niebuhr. To consider a statement—whether factual or moral—true on the basis of religious belief in a personal God is to preclude the possibility of rational argument with those who do not hold the same or any religious convictions. As mentioned before, in a scientific context the word 'objective' is synonymous with 'intersubjective'. Religious faith, feeling, and insight are a profoundly subjective experience and therefore cannot provide an objective ground for moral principles of politics.

III *Based on Rational Insight*

1 / St. Thomas Aquinas

It may seem paradoxical choosing Aquinas to provide the first illustration of intuitionism based on rational insight. Did he not teach, like Augustine, that all knowledge is knowledge of God, and that this knowledge is based on faith? Aquinas distinguishes between supernatural knowledge derived from faith and natural knowledge based on sense experience and reason. The same truth can be known both in the light of divine revelation and by the light of natural reason. While this latter source of knowledge can attain to only a partial sector of the truth, it can do so on its own, unaided by faith, thereby being available to all men, including pagans. Knowledge does not presuppose faith; on the contrary, supernatural knowledge presupposes natural knowledge because revealed truth would be unintelligible without some intellectual effort. Faith never contradicts reason; faith confirms reason, but reaches further.

We have seen that Aquinas does not distinguish between laws in the descriptive and the prescriptive sense. The whole universe is "ruled" by the "eternal law" which is divine reason. Unlike all other objects and creatures which comply unconsciously with the eternal law, man is endowed with reason and free will. He has the choice either to follow or to violate the eternal law. And to comply with it, he must know it.

In order, therefore, that man may know without any doubt what he ought to do and what he ought to avoid, it was necessary for man to be directed in his proper acts by a law given by God, for it is certain that such a law cannot err. (*S.T.*, I–II, Q.91, A.4)

The eternal law, insofar as it determines what is right and wrong for man's free actions, is the natural law. Accordingly,

the light of natural reason, whereby we discern what is good and what is evil, which is the function of the natural law, is nothing else than an imprint on us of the divine light. It is therefore evident that the natural law is nothing else than the rational creature's participation of the eternal law. (Q.91, A.2)

Even though Aquinas uses the Augustinean picture of the divine "imprint," he holds, contrary to Augustine, that the principles of right and wrong, embodied in the natural law, are among the things which man can know by his own reason. Actions are not right or wrong because God commands or prohibits them; God commands what is objectively right and prohibits what is objectively wrong. It is true that

> no one can know the eternal law as it is in itself, except God and the blessed who see God in His essence. But every rational creature knows it according to some reflection, greater or less. . . . Now all men know the truth to a certain extent, at least as to the common principles of the natural law. (Q.93, A.2)

Aquinas distinguishes between speculative and practical reason. The first principle of speculative reason is that "*the same thing cannot be affirmed and denied at the same time*"; the first principle of practical reason or of natural law is that "*good is to be done and promoted, and evil is to be avoided.*" (Q.94, A.2) How do we know these first principles? By reason, not in the sense of deductive reasoning, since they are "indemonstrable principles," but because they are "self-evident principles," and a proposition is self-evident "if its predicate is contained in the notion of the subject." (Q.94, A.2) Such a proposition is usually considered analytic or logically necessary; Aquinas himself states that the first principles of both speculative and practical reason are "necessarily true." (Q.91, A.4)

From the first indemonstrable but self-evident principles of speculative reason, "we draw the conclusions of the various sciences, the knowledge of which is not imparted to us by nature, but acquired by the efforts of reason." (Q.91, A.3) These "proper conclusions, like the universal principles, contain the truth without fail," (Q.94, A.4) since the former can be derived from the latter by purely deductive reasoning. For example, "it is true for all that the three angles of a triangle are together equal to two right angles, although it is not known to all," (*Ibid.*) because some lack the necessary mathematical instruction. Here again, Aquinas draws an analogy between speculative and practical reason.

"All other precepts of the natural law are based upon"
its first principle. (Q.94, A.2)

So too it is that from the precepts of the natural law, as
from common and indemonstrable principles, the human
reason needs to proceed to the more particular determination of certain matters. These particular determinations,
devised by human reason, are called human laws. (Q.91,
A.3)

By "human law," Aquinas does not mean positive law,
but those of the more particular rules of the natural law
which forbid the more grievous offenses such as murder
or theft. His general definition of law—"an ordinance
of reason for the common good, promulgated by him
who has the care of the community" (Q.90, A.4)—applies then especially to the human law.

Unlike the first self-evident principles of speculative
and practical reason and like the "conclusions of the
various sciences," the "particular determinations" of the
law are arrived at by the efforts of human reason. And
just as not all men know the theorems which follow
from the axioms of geometry, not all are endowed with
sufficient reason to know the "peculiar and proper" aspects of the natural law.

But there is one important difference between speculative and practical reason. The conclusions of the sciences, although not known to all, do follow deductively
from the first principles and are, like the former, universally and necessarily true. On the other hand,

something may be derived from the natural law in two
ways: first, as a conclusion from principles; secondly, by
way of a determination of certain common notions. The
first way is like to that by which, in the sciences, demon
strated conclusions are drawn from the principles . .
e.g., that *one must not kill* may be derived as a conclusion
from the principle that *one should do harm to no man*
(Q.95, A.2)

Another example: Just as the theorem of angles in a triangle is true for everyone, "it is right and true for all to act according to reason, and from this principle it follows, as a proper conclusion, that goods entrusted to another should be restored to their owner." (Q.94, A.4) As to derivations from the natural law "by way of a determination" rather than as a "conclusion," Aquinas gives the following example: "The law of nature has it that the evil-doer should be punished, but that he be punished in this or that way is a determination of the law of nature." (Q.95, A.2)

Thus, *rational insight* enables us to know the first principles both of speculative and of practical reason; and *deductive reasoning* makes it possible, after proper training, to arrive at the "conclusions of the various sciences" and at *some* of the more specific principles of natural law.

Aquinas' distinction between indemonstrable first principles and conclusions might be interpreted as referring to the familiar distinction between the axioms and the theorems of a deductive system such as that of Euclidean geometry. The former are statements assumed to be true without demonstration within the given system—e.g., that the shortest distance between two points is a straight line; the latter are logically derivable from the axioms—e.g., the angle theorem to which Aquinas refers. If one presents logic as a deductive system, then Aquinas is correct when he states that the principle of noncontradiction (a statement and its denial cannot both be true) may be considered a first principle or an axiom of logic, which as such functions as an *indemonstrable* assumption from which other principles of logic may be derived as theorems. One may, however, construct equivalent systems of logic based on different sets of axioms in which the rule of noncontradiction can be derived and, hence, *demonstrated* as a theorem. Similarly, if one takes the injunction that good should be done as a first principle of natural law, then it is as such an indemonstrable principle of the system of natural law, i.e., not a theorem but an axiom.

We may also agree with Aquinas that the principle of noncontradiction is logically *necessary* or analytic, since its denial would be contradictory. For the same reason, the first principle of natural law is necessarily true, provided the expression 'x is good' is taken to mean or at least to imply that x should be done. If so, then the predicate of that principle is indeed contained in the notion of the subject; hence, to deny it would involve a self-contradiction. Of course, to show that a statement is necessary or analytic is itself a demonstration, but it is not a demonstration within the system, e.g., of logic or of natural law.

If the first principles of speculative and of practical reason are logically necessary, they are also self-evident in Aquinas' sense, since, as we saw, he uses both terms interchangeably. Aquinas also considers them to be self-evident, at least "to the wise" (Q.94, A.2), in the sense that they can be known through direct rational insight. This may be interpreted to mean that the denial of these principles is not merely self-contradictory, but even inconceivable.

Let us grant that the principle that good is to be done and evil avoided is self-evident as well as logically necessary. Indeed, if by 'good' is meant what ought to be done, then it is self-evident that one ought to do whatever is good. But now the question arises: Is it a principle of practical reason? Is it a moral principle at all? Surely, the answer is "No." It does not enjoin anyone to do this or forbid him to do that; it provides no guidance whatsoever of what ought to be done in any specific situation. If the gas chambers are good, then the Nazi "did good." It is not even possible to conceive of an action which would violate the "command" that good ought to be done, for the very reason that it is self-evident, logically necessary—and vacuous. Conversely f it were a substantive moral principle, it would not be logically necessary, since there exists no genuine normative or valuational judgment whose denial would involve a self-contradiction. Aquinas has not shown that there is a *moral* principle which is necessary, let alone self-evident, because it cannot be shown any more than that the circle can be squared.

Let us now examine those statements which, Aquinas claims, can be known to be true by "reason" in the sense of deductive reasoning rather than of rational insight. The angle theorem can indeed be logically derived from the axioms of Euclidean geometry and is, therefore, a "proper conclusion" within the Euclidean system. The same is true of any theorem within a given deductive system, but not, incidentally, of the "conclusions of the various sciences"; while some empirical laws can be derived from more general ones, their truth depends always on empirical evidence. Nor can a normative statement be logically derived from another normative statement without reference to some further premise (except in trivial cases). (See Chap. 2, I, 3, b) Consequently, even if: 'avoid evil!' were a genuine moral norm, no other substantive moral rule would logically follow from this "first principle of natural law." Yet, according to Aquinas, the command: 'do not do evil!' entails: 'do not harm anyone!' which in turn entails: 'do not kill anyone!' It was mentioned before that, in order to derive the third statement from the second, we need the additional, if rather trivial, premise that to kill someone is to harm him. But to derive the second statement from the first, we must make the further, and far from trivial, assumption that to harm anyone is to do evil. This premise constitutes, in turn, a *moral* principle; and Aquinas tacitly assumes it without showing that it is true. Nor could it be shown to be true by claiming that it is necessary, let alone self-evident. In fact, harming or even killing certain kinds of people— enemies, Jews, slaves, deformed infants, old persons—

has been considered good and right in many ethical sys
tems. Similarly—to take Aquinas' other example—from
the principle that one should act according to reason, i
does not follow "as a proper conclusion" that borrowed
goods should be restituted, unless it is assumed, in addi
tion, that to do so is an act of reason; and as this pre
sumably means that acting this way is morally right, th
argument becomes circular.

As to those moral principles which, according t
Aquinas, are derivable from the first principles of natu
ral law "by way of a determination" and not "as
conclusion," the question arises as to what sort of log
cal relationship this is supposed to be. Either q is log
cally derivable from p or it is not. There are no degree
of logical entailment.* Furthermore, if p does entail q
the logical relationship holds, regardless of whether
not it is, in fact, known to all. If the natural law doe
not specify the penalties for criminal offenses, then it
logically arbitrary which penalties to enact. The choic
of a certain penalty may or may not be *rational*, but th
involves factual, not logical, considerations. Howeve
"determination" may also be interpreted as referring t
the end to which everything naturally tends and whic
human reason is capable of apprehending. This is
different approach to the knowledge of the natural lav
and I shall deal with this part of Aquinas' metaethics i
the next chapter, on naturalism.

In conclusion, I shall give an example of contemp
rary Thomistic reasoning applied to a concrete politic
issue. My purpose is to illustrate that the influence
this thirteenth-century philosopher on certain presen
day political and legal thinkers has remained all-powe
ful and that the question of the validity of his metaeth
cal arguments is by no means of mere historical interes
In the *Fordham Law Review* article quoted below v

* There is a sense of partial implication which is used in pro
abilistic logic, but this is obviously not the sense that Aquinas h
in mind.

are led from the basic principle of natural law that good is to be done by successive steps to the conclusion that making divorce legal is contrary to natural law. (I have italicized expressions characterizing the relationships which are supposed to hold between the various principles.) Whether or not the reasoning of this passage can stand up against the criticisms made in this section is up to the reader to decide.

Natural law is that objective, eternal and immutable hierarchy of moral values, which are sources of obligation with regard to man because they have been so ordained by the Creator of nature. . . . Although this law is divine in the sense that it does not depend on human will, nevertheless, . . natural law is discoverable by reason alone. . . .

The most basic ideal of this law, namely, that every man must live in accordance with his rational nature, so that he will do good and avoid evil, is *self-evident to all.* No reasoning is required to reach a knowledge of this ideal. But other parts of the natural law are not perceivable with an equal degree of facility. *Varying gradations and types of reasoning* are necessary to ascertain the sub-norms of that law. Some of these are discoverable by an immediately derived deduction, which is *almost* obvious, such as the requirement of *some* form of marriage or contractual agreement before a man and a woman can lawfully have sexual relations. But other sub-norms are ascertainable only after observation, study, and experience, both individual and sociological. . . .

The necessity of some kind of marriage, either polygamous or monogamous, dissoluble or indissoluble, is obviously *deducible* from the basic ideal of the natural law, since without propagation and the rearing of children the human race would become extinct. . . .

The characteristics of unity and indissolubility in regard to marriage are secondary conclusions from the natural law, like the right of a worker to a living wage. They are *not readily obvious* . . . . *Reasoning and study* are required to [recognize that] lifelong monogamy is morally necessary for the attainment of man's ethical life, . . .

It is not necessary to have recourse to the rational faculty of deduction and induction, to any considerable extent, to know that polyandry, like murder, may never be reconciled with any part of the natural law under any circumstances. . . .

But while reason does not positively enable man to discover the supernatural law in regard to the marriage bond, it will make known that marriage is a social institution, so that civil authority, exercised by the State, has some jurisdiction over the natural bond in the case of the unbaptized. . . .

The State has the right and duty to create a juridical institution of marriage for the unbaptized, and also for the baptized insofar as the purely civil effects are concerned. . . .

But it has no power to dissolve the marriage bond, which is never civil, but either natural or supernatural. Every positive law which purports to confer authority to grant divorce, except in cases coming within the operation of the supernatural law, is contrary to the natural law, and therefore lacks the element of juridicity. (Brown, pp. 128–133)

2 / Hugo Grotius and John Locke

Grotius reaffirms Aquinas' rationalistic conception of natural law in a more explicit and secularized form. Natural law is a strictly deductive system, like arithmetic and geometry. Its theorems follow logically from its axioms, and these are analytic and self-evident and can as such be apprehended by rational insight.

I have made it my concern to refer the proofs of things touching the law of nature to certain fundamental conceptions which are beyond question, so that no one can deny them without doing violence to himself. (*De Jure Belli a Pacis*, Prolegomena, 39)

In an age of religious disunity and divided ecclesiastical authority, God is no longer considered the omnipotent legislator of Scriptural revelation. Even God's will and power are restricted by the laws of logical necessity, and not even He can alter them. The passage quoted on p. 43 states that the quality of moral baseness or moral *necessity* of an action is determined by right *reason*, and that—so this passage continues—"in consequence, such an act is either forbidden or enjoined by the author of nature, God." In contrast especially to Augustine, Grotius denies that God's will is all-powerful, since He could not have enacted principles of natural law which are self-contradictory.

Measureless as is the power of God, nevertheless it can be said that there are certain things over which that power does not extend. . . . Just as even God, then, cannot cause that two times two should not make four, so He cannot cause that that which is intrinsically evil be not evil. (I, i, x, 5)

What we have been saying would have a degree of validity even if we should concede that which cannot be conceded without the utmost wickedness, that there is no God, or that the affairs of men are of no concern to Him. (Prolegomena, 11)

In other words, even if there were no God, there still would be the same, logically necessary and self-evident, natural law.

That compacts are to be adhered to is just such a self-evident axiom, from which certain theorems of natural law can be logically derived, such as the obligation of rulers to abide by their treaties, of citizens to observe the social covenant with their sovereign and, hence, to obey the latter's enactments, and of individuals to carry out their contractual obligations. Positive law, too, must be understood as a system of abstract and general rules, without reference to contingent matters. "With all truthfulness I aver that, just as mathematicians treat their figures as abstracted from bodies, so in treating law I have withdrawn my mind from every particular fact." (Prolegomena, 58)*

The criticism of Aquinas' metaethical views applies

* In certain other passages, Grotius uses naturalistic arguments.

equally to Grotius' system of natural law. One normative statement cannot be derived from a given normative statement alone. Basic principles to the effect that actions of a certain kind are morally right or wrong are never self-evident since it is always possible to conceive of some contradictory principle which may be affirmed without self-contradiction. The analogy between basic principles of natural law and axioms of Euclidean geometry would, therefore, not hold, even if the latter were self-evident. Until the middle of the nineteenth century, the denial of, say, the axiom that parallel lines never meet was, indeed, considered inconceivable. Since then, however, non-Euclidean geometries have been constructed in which this proposition is neither an axiom nor a theorem and, consequently, not only not self-evident but even demonstrably false.

Locke, since he holds that knowledge of the natural law can be gained by considering either "natural reason . . . or revelation" (*Civil Government*, 25), is, in a sense, closer to Aquinas than is Grotius. Man's actions, including legislative acts, ought to conform "to the law of nature, i.e., to the will of God, of which that is a declaration." (*Civil Government*, 135) On the other hand, "reason, which is that law, teaches all mankind who will but consult it" (*Civil Government*, 6) that all men have the same natural rights. Consequently,

it is certain there is such a law, and that, too, as intelligible and plain to a rational creature and a studier of that law as the positive laws of commonwealths; nay, possibly plainer, as much as reason is easier to be understood than the fancies and intricate contrivances of men. (*Civil Government* 12)

It is with respect to the content of the natural law that Locke differs from Aquinas. According to Locke its basic principle is that of human equality—that all men have the same natural rights, which government have the duty to protect. Like Aquinas, Grotius, and "the judicious Hooker," Locke holds the fundamental principle of natural law to be "evident in itself and beyond all question." (*Civil Government*, 5) But it is not clear whether Locke considers it self-evident for the same reason as does Aquinas; namely, that it is a logically necessary proposition. Possibly Locke regards it as a synthetic proposition, i.e., more like a factual statement which is so evident that reason can apprehend it and that to doubt it or even to conceive of its denial is psychologically impossible. The same ambiguity arises with respect to the "self-evident truths" of the Declaration of Independence or Walter Lippmann's "rational order of human society . . . [which] all men, when they are sincerely or lucidly rational, will regard . . . as self-evident." (see p. 44) If such passages refer to psychological self-evidence, we need only to remember the attacks on Galileo and Darwin to realize that a statement cannot be shown to be true by reference to the fact that it is (at some time) generally and unquestionably believed to be true and that nobody could conceive of its being false. Besides, these alleged moral truths have been far from self-evident even in this psychological sense; the very fact that they had to be proclaimed as self-evident over and over again indicates that there could be and has been disagreement as to their truth and even as to the desirability of their implementation.

From self-evident principles (in whatever sense), Locke derives moral theorems, again like Aquinas or Grotius. Thus, in *An Essay Concerning Human Understanding*, Locke affirms the possibility of establishing

such foundations of our duty and rules of action as might place morality amongst the sciences capable of demonstration: Wherein I doubt not but from self-evident propositions by necessary consequences, as incontestable as those in mathematics, the measures of right and wrong might be made out to anyone that will apply himself with the same indifferency and attention to the one as he does to the other of these sciences. (IV, iii. 18)

He gives the following two examples:

Where there is no property there is no injustice, is a proposition as certain as any demonstration in Euclid: for the idea of property being a right to anything, and the idea to which the name injustice is given being the invasion or violation of that right, it is evident that these ideas being thus established, and these names annexed to them, I can as certainly know this proposition to be true, as that a triangle has three angles equal to two right ones. Again: No government allows absolute liberty; the idea of government being the establishment of society upon certain rules or laws which require conformity to them, and the idea of absolute liberty being for anyone to do whatever he pleases, I am as capable of being certain of the truth of this proposition as of any in the mathematics. (*Ibid.*)

True, both propositions: 'where there is no property there is no injustice' and 'no government allows absolute liberty' are "necessary consequences," not, however, of "self-evident propositions" but of the following *definitions*: 'property' is synonymous with 'right' (Locke does use the term 'property' in this general sense in his writings); 'injustice' (taken here in the sense of an illegal action) is defined as 'an action which violates a property right, i.e., any right'; 'government' means the same as: 'a system of enforceable legal prohibitions' (in contradistinction to anarchy); 'absolute liberty' means that one may act as one pleases without encountering a legal obstacle. Given these definitions, the two propositions are demonstrably true, just as given the definition: 'bachelor = unmarried man', it follows that no bachelor is married; and just as the injunction 'one ought to do good' follows from the definition 'good = what ought to be done'. However, a definition is a logically arbitrary decision or stipulation how to use a certain expression. A definition may conform more or less to common usage or be more or less practical, but a definition is not true or false, let alone logically necessary or self-evident. Furthermore, Locke's two derived propositions do not stipulate "measures of right or wrong," any more than Aquinas' first principle of practical reason. They inform us that in a society without laws, such as the state of nature, no actions are illegal (or legal, one may add) and that every legal prohibition restricts liberty. This is true indeed—by definition. Locke has not made good his claim that there are principles of *morality* which are either themselves self-evident or can be derived from them.

Yet both of these views are maintained even today. For example:

I know the reality of obligations and goodness with as much self-evidence as I know the logical, geometrical, or causal [sic!] necessitations. . . . I cannot doubt the obligation to keep promises or to spare unnecessary pain. (Carritt, p. 43)

The term Natural Law is defined as that self-evident law which, . . . remains essentially—that is to say as to its very foundation and justification—independent of convention or tradition. (Chroust, p. 70)

The Socratic principle that "it is better to suffer wrong than to do wrong" has been compared to Euclid's angle theorem—a "rational truth . . . beyond agreement, dispute, opinion, or consent" because "its underlying principle is the axiom of noncontradiction—the thief contradicts himself because he wants to keep the stolen goods as his property." (Arendt, pp. 14 and 18) However, the thief, were he concerned with morality (most thieves are not), could justify his stealing and keeping the stolen goods by referring to the principle that it is morally right for the poor to take from the rich, to mention only one possibility which involves no self-contradiction. It may seem more plausible to consider a principle such as: 'murder is wrong' to be self-evident in an analytic sense. It would, indeed, be self-contradictory to deny this principle and to affirm that murder is sometimes right—but only if 'murder' is taken as a synonym of 'wrongful killing'. To kill an attacker in self-defense or an enemy in battle or to carry out the death penalty (when legally inflicted) is in general not considered murder. On the other hand, to kill aged parents or sick infants or heretics is judged morally right in some societies and murder in others. The moral statement that such killings are wrong (and hence, by definition, are instances of murder) is not analytic; it cannot be true on purely logical grounds.

3 / Immanuel Kant and Kurt Baier

Kant's philosophy is probably the outstanding example of the claim that there are moral principles which are true *a priori*. They are considered true not on the basis of moral or religious insight but because they are rationally demonstrable. We shall not take up the whole of Kant's moral philosophy, but only his categorical imperative, and only one of its versions. Kant maintains that it is logically impossible for a rational person to adopt a principle of action unless it can, without inconsistency, be adopted by everyone else.

There is, therefore, only one categorical imperative. It is: Act only according to that maxim by which you can at the same time will that it should become a universal law. (*Metaphysics of Morals*, ii)

This categorical imperative is, according to Kant, rationally demonstrable and, for this reason, morally binding on all rational beings. "All imperatives of duty can be derived from this one categorical imperative as a principle." (*Ibid.*) Compatibility with the one categorical imperative is therefore a *sufficient* condition for any principle of action to be a true moral one. Conversely, it is demonstrably inconsistent, irrational, and immoral for anyone to propose that he himself act on a principle if he cannot will that everybody else should also act upon it. Hence, it is demonstrably immoral to permit killing or stealing or slavery, under whatever circumstances, or to adopt any maxim contrary to the golden rule.

In this version at least, the categorical imperative turns out to be nothing but the principle of universalizability. Now, we have seen (Chap. 2, I, 3, b) that this is a purely formal requirement which is satisfied by every imaginable normative principle. Indeed, whoever claims that it is morally right for him to act in some specified way implicitly stipulates that it is right for anyone else in a relevantly similar situation to act in a similar way. The categorical imperative rules out as immoral only two kinds of behavior, not acting on any principle at all (i.e., acting erratically) and making distinctions among persons. Not even the rule: *quidquid principi placuit legis habet vigorem* violates the principle of universalizability (and, hence, the categorical imperative) since it stipulates that *any* person who holds the office of king has the moral and legal right to act as he pleases, and his subjects the moral and legal duty to submit to his pleasure.* To apply a moral principle with distinction of persons does not imply treating all persons equally.

Furthermore, to make no exceptions to a principle does not exclude the adoption of *principles* of exception. To take a previous example: 'stealing is wrong, except if the thief is indigent and his victim very wealthy'.

* This is a general *moral* principle since it has the form: 'For all x, if x has property P (e.g., being a king), then x has the moral right Q'. See Brandt, 1959, p. 19: "By a 'general' ethical statement, we mean two things. First, it is universal, in the sense that it is a statement about *every* case of a certain sort, or about *everybody*. . . . Second, it makes no reference to individuals, but is concerned only with properties." This point was already made by Rousseau: "When I say that the object of laws is always general, I mean that law considers subjects *en masse* and actions in the abstract, and never a particular person or action. Thus the law may indeed decree that there shall be privileges, but it cannot confer them on anybody by name." (*Social Contract*, II, vi)

It is neither logically impossible, nor irrational, nor contrary to the categorical imperative for someone to "will" that this principle be universally adopted. Nor does a slaveholder violate the categorical imperative if he favors the universal adoption of the institution of slavery, at the risk that he might himself become a slave.

So, if the categorical imperative is logically true and rationally demonstrable, it is so at the price of utter vacuity. It is a formal, not an ethical principle, and no substantive moral norms, such as the golden rule, can be shown to be either compatible or incompatible with the principle of universalizability. This criticism of Kant was already made by John Stuart Mill:

When he begins to deduce from this precept any of the actual duties of morality, he fails, almost grotesquely, to show that there would be any contradiction, any logical (not to say physical) impossibility, in the adoption by all rational beings of the most outrageously immoral rules of conduct. All he shows is that the *consequences* of their universal adoption would be such as no one would choose to incur. (*Utilitarianism,* i)

Or rather, such as *some* would not choose to incur them. For example, if I wanted everybody to act on the principle that it is morally permissible to break promises, there would be no mutual trust, and this consequence would be detrimental to some, or perhaps to many, including myself. But Kant does not show that adopting such a maxim is logically impossible, objectively irrational, and demonstrably immoral.

As a modern example of the Kantian view that certain moral principles can be shown to be true on rational grounds, I shall take Kurt Baier's challenging book *The Moral Point of View,* which bears the significant subtitle *A Rational Basis of Ethics.* Widely discussed by philosophers, this book seems to me to have been undeservedly neglected by political scientists even though it deals, at least implicitly, with important problems of social and political ethics.

Aligning himself firmly with value-cognitivism, Baier declares that "there are absolute moral truths, independent of social changes," (p. 235) and that "our moral convictions are true if they can be seen to be required or acceptable *from the moral point of view*." (p. 184)

I take it as established, then, that it is the very meaning of 'a morality' that it should contain a body of moral convictions which can be true or false, that is, a body of rules or precepts for which there are certain tests. (pp. 179–180)

How does one determine whether a moral conviction satisfies the objective criteria of the moral point of view?

Proceeding by elimination, Baier provides two arguments to demonstrate that egoism "is not the point of view of morality." (p. 189) First: The view that everybody may pursue his own interest provides no answer to the question whose interest ought to prevail in cases of conflicts of interest.

But by 'the moral point of view' we *mean* a point of view which is a court of appeal for conflicts of interest. Hence it cannot (logically) be identical with the point of view of self-interest. . . . Moral talk is impossible for consistent egoists. But this amounts to a *reductio ad absurdum* of consistent egoism. (pp. 189–190)

Second: Pursuing one's own interest is an aim, not a principle; but to adopt the moral point of view is to act on principle. "This involves conforming to the rules whether or not doing so favors one's own or anyone else's aim." (p. 191) A principle in the moral sense is not merely a rule which allows no exception—the egoist does fulfill this condition. By their very nature, moral principles

are binding on everyone alike quite irrespective of what are the goals or purposes of the person in question. Hence self-interest cannot be the moral point of view, for it sets every individual one supreme goal, his own interest, which overrules all his other maxims. (p. 195)

If egoism is not a moral principle, there is only one other alternative: rules which are "*for the good of everyone alike.*" (p. 200) They are the ones which correspond to the moral point of view. This general criterion yields conditions such as the "reversibility" of moral rules; "that is, that the behavior in question must be acceptable to a person whether he is at the 'giving' or 'receiving' end of it." (p. 202) Hence, killing, hurting, deceiving are immoral acts. It also yields principles which are relevant to life in society; e.g., to refrain from behavior which becomes harmful to others if a great number of people engage in it (an example would be to waste water when there is a shortage). Baier considers this rule an application of Kant's categorical imperative, to act only on that maxim whereby you can at the same time will that it should become a universal law. (p. 209)

Why should I be moral in the sense of Baier's criterion? This means the same as: How can one prove that I should aim at the good of everybody alike rather than at maximizing my own interest?

The very *raison d'être* of a morality is to yield reasons which overrule the reasons of self-interest in those cases where everyone's following self-interest would be harmful to everyone. *Hence* moral reasons are *superior* to all others. (p. 309)

Why? Because "we can see" that a world in which everyone acts on moral principles "is the better world," and "we can see" that a world in which everyone aims at his own interest "would be the sort which Hobbes describes as the state of nature." (p. 310) It is true that

a person might do better for himself by following enlightened self-interest rather than morality. It is not possible,

however, that *everyone* should do better for himself by following enlightened self-interest rather than morality. The
best possible life *for everyone* is possible only by everyone's
following the rules of morality, that is, rules which quite
frequently may require individuals to make genuine sacri-
fices. (pp. 314–315)

It is true that the principle that it is right for everyone to pursue his interest does not provide an explicit
standard for the resolution of conflicts of interest. Implicitly, however, it stipulates that, if A can make his
interest prevail over B's, or B over A's, he is morally
permitted to do so by whatever means. The result may
be a Hobbesian war of all against all, but not necessarily so. It may also happen that the strongest individual
or group succeeds in ending the state of war by subju-
gating all weaker members of the society. Anarchy or
tyranny may be considered undesirable, but Baier has
not *demonstrated* that such states of affairs are objectively immoral. Nor has he proven that egoism cannot
be a moral point of view; certainly, the statement that
everyone may fight for his own interest and "winner
take all" is a *moral* principle (and not a factual one).
Its adoption (at least by the weak) may be irrational
but involves no self-contradiction; that egoists must
fight it out and cannot talk it out does not amount to
a *reductio ad absurdum* of consistent egoism.

From the point of view of political science, there is
the further criticism that egalitarian utilitarianism is not
the only possible alternative to egoism. A significant
third possibility is the *moral* point of view of *elitism*
which holds that it is morally right for a social or political system to promote the interest of some privileged
group (or to allow that group to pursue its interests)
while all other members of the society have the moral
duty to serve the interests of the former. This extreme
form of inegalitarianism has, in fact, been the principle
underlying a great many systems of political ethics, and
it has been the practice of an even greater number of all

known societies. That political institutions ought to promote the good of everyone *alike* has been, especially if taken literally, the ethical conviction of a minority.

It is correct that to adopt the moral point of view is to adopt universal moral *principles*. But here the criticism made of Kant's categorical imperative applies again. This requirement is satisfied by *every* principle of action, e.g., by the principle that persons of certain hereditary status or religion or color are entitled to oppress all who lack such characteristics and that the latter are bound to obey the former. This is a *moral* principle, and it may even fulfill the condition of reversibility. Indeed, the oppressed often approve of the policies of which they are the victims.

Baier's reason for the "superiority" of egalitarian utilitarianism over egoism is that the former brings about a "better world" than the latter. Presumably, he would have used the same argument to prove that the former is superior to elitism, had he dealt with this alternative. But he has not *demonstrated* that it is a better world. All he has said is that "we can see" that it is.

Baier adds nothing to his argument by using the terms 'moral' and 'principle' persuasively to apply only to those moral principles of which he happens to approve. If egoism and inegalitarianism are not moral principles—however immoral they may be considered—then what are they?

4

Naturalism as a Political Philosophy

I Based on Empirical Generalizations

The metaethics of naturalism denies that "values" can be apprehended directly by means of an alleged sixth, moral sense or through religious faith or rational insight. Instead, this theory, in its simpler form, holds that valuational and ethical principles can be *derived* from descriptive generalizations which, in turn, can be *empirically* verified. Historically, this type of naturalism did not become prevalent until the middle of the nineteenth century, when the enthusiasm for "scientific method" reached its height. The natural sciences were the first to come to maturity, which may explain why physical, and especially biological, laws have been so often adopted as premises for moral conclusions in modern times, especially in the area of politics.

1 / Herbert Spencer

"My ultimate purpose, lying behind all proximate purposes, has been that of finding for the principles of right and wrong, in conduct at large, a scientific basis." (*Data of Ethics*, Preface, p. vii) Spencer believed that he had found in the theory of evolution (which he formulated before Darwin) the scientific basis for right conduct at large, and more particularly for right governmental policy. He considered evolution to be the single principle capable of explaining and predicting all observable phenomena and, hence, of unifying all sciences, from astronomy via physics and biology to psychology, sociology, and politics—and ethics as well. Whether we consider the solar system or the geological structure of the earth or any biological or social organism, they all are characterized by growth, differentiation of function, and increasing complexity of structure. Life is a continuous process of adaptation to external environment. Plants, animals, human individuals, and societies are all engaged in a permanent competitive struggle for survival. Those who adapt themselves successfully to the environment tend to survive; those unable to adapt are bound to perish. Evolution is adaptation, adaptation is a struggle for existence, and natural selection results in the survival of the fittest.

In our modern industrial and commercial society, the "fittest" are those capable of taking the fullest advantage of their economic, social, and political environment—the physically and mentally healthy, the intelligent, the industrious, the thrifty. Accepting Lamarck's theory of the inheritance of acquired characteristics, Spencer predicted that those who win out in the competition will transmit their character traits to succeeding generations, while the sick, the poor, the stupid, the lazy will gradually disappear. Thus, the human race is bound to improve not only physically and intellectually but morally as well. Egoism, a characteristic of primitive men in a predatory society, is also necessary for survival in this current age of competitive capitalism; eventually it will be superseded by the higher morality of benevolence and altruism.

Adopting the organic view of society, Spencer held that social organisms, too, participate in the general evolutionary process. "Instead of civilization being artificial, it is a part of nature; all of a piece with the development of the embryo or the unfolding of a flower." (*Social Statics*, ii, 4) Scarcity of resources in relation to increase of population promotes technological innovation and scientific discoveries leading to higher civilization. Wars between social organisms will eventually be superseded by universal social cooperation. Government is necessary only because and as long as men retain their primitive egoistic instincts. Its function is to prevent citizens from encroaching upon each other's basic rights, not to interfere in their ongoing struggle for survival. With the gradual change from egoism to benevolence, governmental coercion will become increasingly superfluous and will disappear altogether with the emergence of the ideal man and the ideal society which will realize the utilitarian goal of happiness for all.

Historical as well as biological evolution is then a necessary process which cannot be hastened or slowed down, let alone altered by human intervention. Spencer was more than a determinist, a fatalist who denied that men can influence the inevitable, lawful course of historical evolution. "The ultimate development of the ideal man is logically certain—as certain as any conclusion in which we place the most implicit faith; for instance, that all men will die." (*Ibid*. Spencer means, of course, empirically, rather than logically, certain.)

How are Spencer's factual generalizations connected with his value judgments and with his normative principles? There is a strict parallelism between facts and values. Evolution is not only a *process* in time but also a *progress* toward perfection. "Evolution can end only in the establishment of the greatest perfection and the most complete happiness." (*First Principles*, xxii, 176) Consequently, any event which contributes to the evolutionary process has positive value. The weeding-out of the unfit promotes evolution toward ultimate perfection and is, therefore, beneficial, however cruel and undesirable it may appear, especially to its victims. Those fit for survival are worthy to survive; the unfit are the unworthy; and it is good that they suffer the evils which they bring on themselves.

Pervading all nature we may see at work a stern discipline, which is a little cruel that it may be very kind. That state of universal warfare maintained throughout the lower creation, to the great perplexity of many worthy people, is at bottom the most merciful provision which the circumstances admit of. . . . The poverty of the incapable, the distresses that come upon the imprudent, the starvation of the idle, . . . are the decrees of a large, far-seeing benevolence. (*Social Statics*, xxv, 6)

A happy coincidence indeed! What is bound to happen in any event is also bound to turn out for the best. "Progress is not an accident, not a thing within human control, but a *beneficent necessity*." (*Essays*, Vol. I, p. 60; italics added)

Now, if Spencer holds that the beneficent and good is also necessary and beyond human control, there can be no room in his system for normative principles directing us to realize what is bound to occur regardless of what we do. Yet Spencer does not only proclaim "principles of right and wrong conduct at large," but also endeavors to find for them "a scientific basis."

Spencer advocated that government should confine itself to a single function; namely, to grant to all its citizens equal legal rights and to protect everybody's *"freedom to do all that he wills, provided he infringes not the equal freedom of any other man."* (*Social Stat-*

ics, vi, 1) On the one hand, he championed equality of rights for women and children; on the other, he considered any further extension of the scope of governmental authority morally wrong because it would interfere with the natural struggle for existence and survival of the fittest. Accordingly, government should protect everyone's legal right to accumulate whatever amount of wealth he can but should not itself provide for the satisfaction of even the most basic needs. He did not object to private charity; however, "the assumption by a government of the office of Reliever-general to the poor, is necessarily forbidden by the principle that a government cannot rightly do anything more than protect" (*Social Statics*, xxv, 1)—that is, protect the *right* to acquire the necessities and even the superfluities of life. Taxing the wealthy to help the poor is, therefore, immoral. For the same reason, Spencer opposed taxation for the purpose of setting up a public school system. The children's "rights are not violated by a neglect of their education," (*Social Statics*, xxvi, 1) and it is the duty of government to guarantee equality of rights, but not of opportunity. Legislation regulating conditions of work, safety, sanitation, and housing were equally abhorrent to Spencer, and on the same grounds, namely, "that the quality of society is physically lowered by the artificial preservation of its feeblest members." (*The Study of Sociology*, xiv) As to men in general, "if they are sufficiently complete to live, they *do* live, and it is well they should live. If they are not sufficiently complete to live, they die, and it is best they should die." (*Social Statics*, xxviii, 4)

Let us assume for a moment, for the sake of argument, that Spencer's principle of evolution does pervade all nature, including human life. One might share his satisfaction with this natural state of affairs. One might, accordingly, express the *value* judgment that the actual world is the best of all possible worlds. But there is no point in making a normative judgment to the effect that those fit for survival (and who do survive) *ought* to live and that the others should die or be left to die, just as it would be pointless to *advocate* that all living creatures should breathe. If, on the other hand, the law of evolution does not apply to human individuals, then it is logically and empirically possible either to advocate a *laissez-faire* policy or to hold that government should enable the physically and economically weak to survive. Yet, Spencer wants to have it both ways:

Thus, that which sundry precepts of the current religion embody—that which ethical systems, intuitive or utilitarian, equally urge, is that which Biology also, generalizing the laws of life, dictates. (*The Study of Sociology*, xiv)

As if religion and ethics could urge us to bring about the very state of affairs which the laws of biology predict (not dictate!) will come about in any event. A few sentences further we read:

But unhappily, legislators and philanthropists, busy with schemes which hinder adaptation instead of aiding it, neglect those arrangements by which adaptation is effected. (*Ibid.*)

Suddenly it becomes possible for men or governments either to aid or to hinder adaptation and evolution. It is, after all, up to legislators either to prevent misery now at the risk (or certainty) of greater unhappiness in the future or to be cruel now for the sake of the greater well-being of those who will eventually survive as the result of natural selection. Spencer is not able to demonstrate that the second alternative is intrinsically more desirable than the first.

If we choose as our ultimate goal the greatest possible happiness of future generations, then *laissez faire* could be empirically shown to be desirable instrumentally, provided that the alleged causal connections hold. Evidently, they do not. The laws of evolution, which Darwin applied to *species* of plants and animals, do not hold true for human *individuals*, not even in the weakened form which introduces present governmental policies as a variable influencing the future evolution of mankind. Poverty is more often the result of social circumstances than of individual laziness; it is certainly not an inherited and transmittable biological trait. Furthermore, if social legislation amounts to "fostering the good-for-nothing at the expense of the good, . . . a deliberate storing-up of miseries for future generations" (*Ibid.*), why does private charity not influence the alleged evolutionary process, and why does not every instance of (private or public) medical intervention constitute an immoral interference with the natural and beneficent process of evolution?

If one wants to show that a statement is true by deriving it from other statements, one needs to establish that the premises involved are true and that the inference is valid. We have seen that the descriptive generalizations which serve as Spencer's premises are clearly false. Hence, surely his normative conclusion cannot be said to have been established. At this point we need, therefore, not even concern ourselves with the question whether it is ever possible to infer a moral principle from a descriptive generalization.

Herbert Spencer's evolutionary determinism suggests a comparison with the economic determinism of his contemporary, Karl Marx. Both believed that the future course of history was certain, beyond human control, and would lead to the withering away of the State as an organized political power. Needless to say, Marx's scheme of values was at the opposite pole from Spencer's. More important from the point of view of our topic, Marx's metaethical philosophy was noncognitivistic, not naturalistic, as we shall see. He considered the various systems of morality mere ideological rationalizations of rival class interests, not objectively either true or false. Marx did not hold that the world revolution leading to the classless society ought to be promoted *because* its occurrence is historically necessary. Lenin, on the other hand, said, at least at one point: "Our morality is deduced from the class struggle of the proletariat." (Lenin) Yet Marx was caught in a dilemma similar to Spencer's: If the proletariat will by historical necessity overthrow the bourgeoisie when the situation is ripe, neither sooner nor later, what is the point of urging the workers of all countries to unite to bring about precisely what they will be historically compelled to do?

2 / George G. Simpson

The chapter entitled "The Ethics of Knowledge and Responsibility" in George G. Simpson's book *The Meaning of Evolution* may be taken as an example of more recent attempts to derive moral principles of politics from descriptive principles of evolution. Spencer's cosmic and quasi-metaphysical theory of evolution is here reduced to its scientific proportions by an eminent biologist. Evolution is not a single linear and purposeful progress from amoeba via egoistic man to the future harmonious society. "Man is the result of a purposeless and materialistic process that did not have him in mind. . . . He happens to represent the highest form of organization of matter and energy that has ever appeared." p. 179) The features which set man apart from all other animals are the "interrelated factors of intelligence, flexibility, individualization, and socialization. . . . In man all four are carried to a degree incomparably greater than in any other sort of animal." (p. 138) Man is, to a unique degree, capable of conscious knowledge, deliberate choice, and rational behavior.

The most essential material factor in the new evolution seems to be just this: knowledge, together, necessarily, with its spread and inheritance. As a first proposition of evolutionary ethics *derived from specifically human evolution*, it is submitted that promotion of knowledge is essentially good. (p. 156; italics added)

And since this is a proposition of *ethics*, it follows that knowledge ought to be promoted and that to hinder its diffusion is morally wrong.

Our main criticism of Spencer's argument was that his factual premises are false. Simpson's evolutionary theory, on the other hand, is generally considered true by modern biologists. So the question is: Does a valuational or normative principle ever follow deductively from a factual generalization? Does an assertion to the effect that something is the case ever logically entail that such a state of affairs is intrinsically good and ought to be realized? Clearly, no. Deduction consists merely in making explicit what is implicitly asserted by the premises. Consequently, a premise which does not refer to what is good or right does not entail a conclusion which does. Even if Spencer's descriptive theories were true, they would not entail his normative principles. Simpson's descriptive theory *is* true, but his valuational principle cannot be shown to be true as a logical consequence. From the fact that man has knowledge and that it spreads, it does not follow that its promotion is good and that it is morally right to spread it.

Furthermore, it appears that Simpson, too, is caught in the dilemma: if it is an evolutionary fact that human knowledge does spread, then there is no significance to the "proposition of evolutionary *ethics*" that knowledge ought to be promoted—it will spread in any event, even in political societies which, instead of encouraging its dissemination, restrict freedom of speech. On the other hand, Simpson may be mistaken; knowledge does not necessarily spread; its dissemination may be prevented, e.g., by totalitarian political systems. Only if it is not the case that knowledge is bound to spread does it make sense to proclaim that government ought to further its propagation, and that regimes which do not are morally wrong. Possibly, Simpson means only to assert that the diffusion can never be totally stopped for any length of time without denying that its spread can be either furthered or impeded by political intervention. Then one may hold that the more rapid its diffusion, the better; but this valuational principle cannot be based on the *fact* that knowledge is bound to spread in any event, however slowly.

Simpson's second principle of evolutionary ethics is derived from the "fact" of human responsibility. "Conscious knowledge, purpose, choice, and values carry as an inevitable corollary responsibility." (p. 155)

It is now submitted that the highest and most essential moral ethical standards are involved in the fact of man's personal responsibility. This responsibility is not itself an ethic. It is a fact, a fundamental and peculiar characteristic of the human species established by his evolution and evident in his relationship to the rest of the cosmos. Recognition of this responsibility and its proper exercise are the firm basis on which right and moral human action must be based. . . . It involves responsibilities for every living person, and responsibilities that cannot be ethically evaded; that is, their evasion is morally wrong. (pp. 157–158)

Here, the objection is not only that "moral ethical standards" cannot be derived from a "fact," but also that the factual premise and the ethical conclusion do not even refer to the same state of affairs. The fact that man, and only man, has the capacity of knowledge and purposive behavior "carries as an inevitable corollary responsibility" only in the sense that he is *capable* of acting responsibly; and this means only that he *can* foresee (within limits) the effects of his own conduct, although he does in fact often act irresponsibly, i.e., without foresight. That man *should* take his responsibilities and that "their evasion is morally wrong" means that he should deliberate about the consequences of his conduct before acting, that he should consider himself answerable to society for his actions, and that he should, therefore, refrain from acting in a way which society considers morally blameworthy.

By using 'responsibility' indiscriminately in the sense of acting responsibly and being capable of doing so, Simpson oscillates between 'ought' and 'can', between norms and facts:

Responsibility is rooted in the true nature of man. It has arisen from and is inherent in his evolutionary history and status. Responsibility is something that he has just because he is human, and not something that he can choose to accept or to refuse. It *cannot* be rejected or unconditionally handed over to others. The attempt to do so is ethically *wrong*, and the responsibility remains where it was. . . . The collective aspects of the state *are, or ethically should be*, achieved by means of personal responsibility in all its members. (p. 161; italics added)

[Responsibility] is correlated with another human evolutionary characteristic, that of high individualization. From this relationship arises the ethical judgment that it is good, right, and moral to recognize the integrity and dignity of the individual and to promote the realization or fulfillment of individual capacities. (p. 159)

In other words: human beings are highly differentiated; *therefore*, society ought to protect human dignity and to promote individual self-realization. This leads Simpson to the opposite conclusion of Spencer's evolutionary ethics; namely, that "laissez-faire capitalism . . . is obviously wrong by these standards." (p. 163) Furthermore, "authoritarianism is wrong," because it

involves an attempt to delegate nondelegable responsibility for subsequent actions of the delegate. This is an ethically wrong denial of the personal responsibility inherent in man's nature. (p. 163)

Does 'nondelegable responsibility' mean that it cannot, or that it ought not, be delegated? If the former, how can it be "ethically wrong" to do what cannot be done? If the latter, what is the connection with "man's nature?"

Simpson points out that "these ethical standards are relative, not absolute," in the sense that they are relative to the present state of human evolution, and "subject to future change as man evolves." (p. 165) Simpson would not deny that he considers these ethical standards absolute in another sense; namely, that they are, at any given time of human evolution, based on objective facts. The last sentence of the chapter reads: "These relativistic ethics have, at least, the merit of being honestly derived from what seems to be demonstrably true and clear." (p. 165)

3 / H. L. A. Hart

The objection might be raised that, in choosing Spencer and Simpson as examples of naturalism, we are knocking down straw men and making it too easy for ourselves. The reply is that Spencerian and neo-Spencerian theories have been not only the most representative but also most influential naturalistic theories in recent political philosophy. Let us, however, examine a much more attenuated and, at first glance, much more plausible version of naturalism taken from one of the most lucid recent works in legal philosophy, namely, H. L. A. Hart's *The Concept of Law*.

The author starts from a series of empirical assertions concerning goals which men ordinarily choose and concerning means which must necessarily be used to attain them. There is, first, "the simple contingent fact that most men most of the time wish to continue in existence." (p. 187) As a general rule, men prefer to live, however miserably, and to die a natural death rather than to fall violently at the hand of another. In order to survive, men must live in a society which itself is "viable." And a society cannot survive unless it contains a certain minimum number of rules. Thus, "there are certain rules of conduct which any social organization must contain if it is to be viable." (p. 188) The following are among the moral and legal principles which Hart considers necessary for the survival of society and its members: Given the (contingent) fact that men (unlike shellfish) are vulnerable to attack by members of their own species, it becomes necessary for every society to adopt some sort of rules "that restrict the use of violence in killing or inflicting bodily harm." (p. 190) It is also a fact that the similarities of men's physical strength and intellectual ability are socially more significant than their differences in these respects. "This fact of approximate equality, more than any other, makes obvious the necessity for a system of mutual forbearance and compromise." (p. 191) Furthermore, the necessities of human life are in short supply. "These facts alone make indispensable some minimal form of the institution of property (though not necessarily individual property), and the distinctive kind of rule which requires respect for it." (p. 192)

We come now to the normative aspect of Hart's theory, namely, that "the *proper* end of human activity is survival," and that "the actions . . . which are naturally *good* to do, are those which are required for survival." (p. 187; italics added) It is at least possible to interpret these phrases in the normative sense that survival *ought* to be the end of human activity, and that actions conducive to survival are good because they are means to an end which is itself intrinsically desirable.

This is an ambiguous value judgment. Does it mean that the proper end of every man is his own survival? That everyone ought to aim at the survival of all, or at least of all members of his society? That society as a whole ought to be responsible for protecting the lives of its members? This last interpretation is suggested by the statement that without the above-mentioned rules "laws and morals could not forward the minimum purpose of survival which men have *in associating with each other.*" (p. 189; italics added) Like the classical social contract theorists, Hart compares social and political organizations to voluntary associations, formed to carry out the purposes of all associates, in this case the survival of each. Now, a viable society is a necessary but by no means a sufficient condition for insuring the survival of all. Hart himself acknowledges the fact that, "though a society to be viable must offer *some* of its members a system of mutual forbearances, it need not, unfortunately, offer them to all." (p. 196) There have been stable and enduring social systems which considered the lives of slaves expendable or the survival of the economically weak of no public concern. If someone's goal is his own survival and if he is born into a privileged group, then he will prefer a political system which protects the vested interests of that group. If he desires the survival of all, e.g., because he considers it the "proper end," then it is necessary to have institutions which are not merely viable but also egalitarian.

To examine Hart's metaethical position, I shall cite the full text of a passage already quoted in part. Referring to certain "teleological elements still alive in ordinary thought about human action," he says:

It will be rightly observed that what makes sense in this mode of thought and expression is something entirely obvious: it is the tacit assumption that the proper end of human activity is survival, and this *rests on the* simple contingent *fact that* most men most of the time wish to continue in existence. The actions which we speak of as those which are *naturally* good to do, are those which are required for survival. (p. 187; italics added)

Like Spencer or Simpson, Hart seems to adopt the naturalistic view that a norm can in some way be derived from ("rests on") a fact—a "biological fact which man shares with other animals." (p. 187) Man ought to aim at survival (his own? everyone's?) *because* man does aim at survival. Our general criticism of this approach applies to Hart's theory as well. That man wants to survive does not entail that man ought to aim at his own survival, let alone that the survival of all is the proper, i.e., desirable, end of human activity.

Actions which are required for survival "are naturally good to do." Does this mean that there is a rule of natural law to the effect that survival in some sense ought to be promoted? Hart does characterize his theory as a "very attenuated version of Natural Law" (p. 187)—attenuated because it does not contain such specific injunctions as those of classical natural law but pertains only to the minimum rules necessary to maintain a viable society.

Such universally recognized principles of conduct which have a basis in elementary truths concerning human beings, their natural environment, and aims, may be considered the *minimum content* of Natural Law. (p. 189)

Does Hart mean by 'natural law' the metaethical theory which we have examined in Chapter 2? If so, the objection is that his naturalistic method has not been successful in demonstrating that there are objective principles of natural law, let alone that the injunction to adopt the minimum rules is a principle of natural law. Furthermore, the content of Hart's natural law is merely this: every society *ought* to have rules which protect the life and property of *some* of its members. This is indeed a minimum requirement, so minimal that every social system satisfies it, from the most egalitarian to the most hierarchical. Only anarchy would violate this condition, and anarchy, by definition, does not constitute a social system. So it turns out that these minimum rules, far from being norms of natural law, can hardly be regarded as normative principles at all. They merely enumerate some matters which every social system does in fact regulate—in whatever way it sees fit. This suggests the possibility that Hart uses the term 'natural law' in a sense similar to Hobbes and Hume. (See Chap. 2, II, 3) If so, he merely means to make the factual assertion that men desire to live, and that certain minimum rules *are* required to insure the survival of *any* society and of *some* of its members. Then my objection would be merely terminological. It seems misleading to speak of natural law in a purely empirical context.

In this connection, I shall return briefly to the work of Carl Friedrich. This may seem surprising since I had previously taken his theory as an example of intuitionism based on moral insight. Yet, curiously indeed, Friedrich also uses naturalistic arguments similar to Hart's to establish the objective nature of basic normative principles. "What *ought to be* the model of human effort is derived from what *is* the content of human experience." (Friedrich, p. 658) Note how his factual premise below resembles Hart's.

The basic datum of politics . . . is the fact that men value their life, . . . their communal life as contrasted with their mere physical existence, above all else. It *is* the highest good in the objective sense of empirical *being*, and the precondition of all other experience, political or otherwise. (p. 53)

Two reasons are often less convincing than one. If the highest political values could be directly apprehended through our primary value experiences (see Chap. 3, I, 3), there would be no need to "derive" them from the "basic datum of politics." As to this alleged basic datum itself, it is a fact that most men most of the time desire to preserve their physical life and also (but not necessarily more so) to live in society—of *some* type. However, they are often opposed to the kind of communal life and political system to which they happen to be subjected. Whatever the facts may be, it does not follow that communal life as such "*is* the highest good in the objective sense." Finally, if the highest intrinsic value were assigned to communal life, this would be so general a goal as to be compatible with any conceivable system of political institutions and of political ethics.

4 / Hans Morgenthau

Moral principles of international politics, too, have been defended on the basis of biological and psychological theories of survival. Consider, for example, Hans Morgenthau.

Self-preservation for the individual as well as for societies is not only a biological and psychological necessity, but in the absence of an overriding moral obligation a moral duty as well. . . . A foreign policy derived from the national interest is in fact morally superior to a foreign policy inspired by universal moral principles. (Morgenthau, p. 854)

Morgenthau distinguishes between two kinds of foreign policy goals, pursuing "the national interest" and adopting "universal moral principles." The former includes as a minimum the protection of national security;* the latter refers to such principles as coming to the rescue of any foreign state whose national independence or "free" institutions or ability to determine its own form of government is threatened by aggression from the outside or from within. Every nation has the moral right and even "a positive moral duty" (*Ibid.*) to protect its national security; but it is morally wrong for any state to adopt foreign policy goals based exclusively on moral considerations. The use of military force is, therefore, morally justified provided it is necessary for national self-preservation but morally illegitimate when used for the implementation of "moralistic" goals.

To demonstrate this general moral principle of politics among nations, Morgenthau relies on a negative and on

---

* This is not the place to examine whether it is possible to give an operational definition of the concept of national interest.

a positive argument. "The choice is not between moral principles and the national interest, devoid of moral dignity," (p. 853) but between two sets of principles, both of which are of ethical character. "Hence, the antithesis between moral principles and the national interest is not only intellectually mistaken but also morally pernicious." (p. 854) In other words, it cannot be shown that it is morally wrong to pursue the national interest by denying that it is acting according to a moral principle. This point is well taken. The statement: 'all nations ought to adopt *x* as their foreign policy goal' constitutes an ethical principle whether *x* stands for a so-called moral principle or for the protection of natural security.

But why is the moral principle that nations ought to aim at protecting their national security a *true* one? Why is it *mistaken* to adopt moralistic foreign policy goals? Because the duty to pursue the national interest is "derived from political reality," while moralistic foreign policy principles are "divorced from political reality." And—to repeat Morgenthau's earlier statement— "a foreign policy *derived* from the national interest is *in fact* morally superior to a foreign policy inspired by universal moral principles."

What are the "facts," what is the "political reality" from which the rightness of the pursuit of the national interest is "derived?" Referring to the other statement quoted at the beginning: "Self-preservation . . . for societies is . . . a biological and psychological necessity." There is no effective supranational organization. "For the individual nations to take care of their own national interests is, then, a political necessity." (p. 854)

Here the ambiguous term 'necessity' appears again, as in so many naturalistic metaethical arguments. Morgenthau's assertions about political necessity may be interpreted as follows: moralistic foreign policy goals can be implemented, if at all, only at the price of overcommitment which is bound to weaken national power and to endanger national security; that is why such policies are "divorced from political reality." This leaves as the only alternative the pursuit of the national interest, and national self-preservation is often the only attainable goal, given the necessarily limited power of even the most powerful nations; it is, therefore, a "political necessity" for foreign policy makers to concentrate their efforts on the protection of their nation's security.

One might object that the same policy may serve both types of goals, as illustrated by the participation of the United States in the two World Wars; that "morality" is sometimes "the best policy"; that universal moral principles are often invoked as an ideological justification of "power politics." We may, nevertheless, grant that Morgenthau's thesis is most often borne out by the facts and that it needs to be emphasized, especially in the United States where public opinion and even statesmen tend to favor moralistic foreign policy goals without realizing that their adoption weakens national security.

So far, so good. But what does this prove? Only that it is *irrational* to adopt simultaneously both types of goals, not that it is *immoral* to adopt either. *If* a government is primarily concerned with protecting its national security, then it is irrational to adopt at the same time some conflicting moralistic goal; and a nation which pursues a goal of the latter type must realize that it does so at the risk of endangering its national security.

Yet Morgenthau maintains that it is objectively moral (as well as rational) for nations to pursue their respective national interests, at least as far as required for the protection of national security, and that it is demonstrably immoral (as well as irrational) to adopt moralistic foreign policy goals. This leads to another possible interpretation of Morgenthau's concept of necessity: it is politically necessary for nations to aim at their own preservation, just as it is psychologically necessary for human individuals and biologically necessary for other organisms to survive. While biological organisms behave instinctively, human beings have, at least theoretically, the choice between life and death; and nations, among self-preservation, imperialistic expansion, and surrender of their independence. All Morgenthau presumably means to affirm is that nations do, in fact, always aim at self-preservation as their minimum goal, just as individuals generally want to live (suicide and sacrifice of one's life for others or for some ideal being exceptions). Consequently, if a nation fails to preserve its national identity, it is either because it lacks the power to do so or because it makes wrong foreign policy decisions, such as adopting moralistic goals.

But this is still too sweeping a generalization. It is true that those who wield governmental power are usually interested in maintaining the independence of the state over which they rule. But citizens—individuals and groups—often do not share their government's goal. To Marx, the workers had no fatherland; nationalism was a bourgeois ideology; and class, rather than national, solidarity was what mattered. Nationalists, on the other hand, may want to break up the existing political system into independent units which, they claim, correspond to ethnic realities. Opponents of a political regime may welcome military defeat and loss of national independence to bring about a preferable form of government. Again, the analogy between organic biological units and political systems is misleading. And again, even if self-preservation were a necessity for nations (in any sense of the term), there is no moral principle of politics which could be derived from the alleged fact.

Morgenthau's factual allegations leave me, then, free to adopt any of the following normative positions: (1) Nations generally, or powerful democratic nations such as the United States, ought to be guided in their foreign policy by the above-mentioned moral principle, even at the risk of overcommitting themselves and, hence, o weakening their national security—but not beyond a certain point, after which they would become powerless to implement their moralistic goal in the future. (2) No nation has the moral right to impose its "way of life" on others by force; but every nation has the moral duty to protect its national security, by force if necessary. (3) States having certain characteristics (e.g., a certain type of regime) have no moral right even to defend their national security. (The Nazis held this view of Poland and today some Americans hold this view of China.) (4) It is *desirable* that *certain* countries, e.g., the United States, should preserve their independence, perhaps as a means of preserving American (and generally Western) institutions, culture, and affluence; but such pursuit of the "national interest" is not *morally* right or wrong. (Personally, this is the position I am inclined to take.)

Bertrand Russell once said: "Almost all philosophers, in their ethical systems, first lay down a false doctrine, and then argue that wickedness consists in acting in a manner that proves it false, which would be impossible if the doctrine were true." (Russell, p. 617) This statement applies, if not to almost all moral philosophers, certainly to the naturalistic philosophies of politics we have examined so far.

II *Based on Teleological Generalizations*

1 / Aristotle

A second variety of naturalism has been used by political philosophers long before the present scientific age and goes back to Aristotle. "The good life is the chief end, both for the community as a whole and for each of us individually." (*Politics*, 1278b) This key sentence allows for several different interpretations.

1 It may, first of all, be taken as a genuine factual generalization. Just as Hart asserts that men, generally, aim at preserving their lives, so Aristotle makes the more specific claim that men, and communities as well, choose the good life as their end. This interpretation is borne out by a number of other statements. Thus, Aristotle's *Ethics* and *Politics* both begin with what are clearly empirical generalizations; namely, that "every practical pursuit or undertaking, seems to aim at some good" (*Ethics*, 1094a) and that "observation shows us . . . that . . . all men do all their acts with a view to achieving something which is, in their view, a good." (*Politics*, 1252a) Observation indicates further that what is true of individuals is also true of human associations; namely, that "all associations are instituted for the purpose of attaining some good." (*Ibid.*) So far, we have only been told that men tend to act deliberately in order to realize whatever state of affairs they happen to consider desirable or good. But Aristotle goes on to claim that, while we may desire all sorts of things as a means to something else— e.g., honor, pleasure, intelligence—there is one thing which all of us desire always, and always as an end in itself. This ultimate goal is *eudaimonia*, usually translated as happiness or the good life. "Now happiness above all else appears to be absolutely final in this sense, since we always choose it for its own sake and never as a means to something else." (*Ethics*, 1097b) This is true not only of every person but also of every political community. "The good life is the chief end, both for the community as a whole and for each of us individually."

While we may agree with Hart that men, in general, aim at going on living, it is by no means the case that men always aim at the good life in the sense of happiness. It is even doubtful whether happiness can be considered a goal at all.

2 Aristotle himself seems to realize that 'happiness' is

a rather vague idea. He concedes that agreement as to the chief end of happiness is merely verbal, since some people identify happiness with material goods; others, with the honors of political life; and still others, with intellectual pursuits. (*Ethics*, 1095a) But then 'happiness' comes to designate whatever end anyone adopts. If so, the statement that all seek happiness becomes true, but true by definition. It is no longer a factual assertion but a tautology; it would be just as impossible to find someone not seeking happiness as to find a married bachelor.

3 The terms 'purpose' and 'end' apply, in Aristotle's philosophy, not only to man's deliberate activities but to everything in nature as well. "Nature . . . makes each separate thing for a separate end." (*Politics*, 1252b) A thing's end or purpose or function is, then, determined not by the thing itself, nor by man, nor by some supranatural deity but by nature itself. It is the purpose and function of an acorn to grow into a tree, and the latter is the end or final cause of the former. Not only plants and animals have their respective final ends but also inanimate objects, including human artifacts. Thus, cutting is the purpose not only of the user of a knife but also of the knife itself. Similarly, nature assigns purposes to various organs of animal and human organisms and also to the various kinds of human beings themselves—slaves, women, artisans—independently of their own choices. If so, Aristotle argues, there must also be a function of man as such, beyond the various kinds of ends which various people do, in fact, adopt.

Are we then to suppose that, while the carpenter and the shoemaker have definite functions or businesses belonging to them, man as such has none, and is not designed by nature to fulfill any function? Must we not assume that, just as the eye, the hand, the foot and each of the various members of the body manifestly has a certain function of its own, so a human being also has a certain function over and above all the functions of his particular members? (*Ethics*, 1097b)

Now, a thing's function is what it can do best, or what it alone can do. Consequently, "the function of man is the active exercise of the soul's faculties in conformity with rational principle" (*Ethics*, 1098a); i.e., to think reflectively and to act rationally.

Viewed in the present context, the statement that the good life is the chief end of man acquires a somewhat different, namely, teleological, meaning: while men do, as a matter of fact, pursue various goals under the guise of happiness, the contemplative life is the only kind of happiness which nature has assigned to man as its real purpose or final end. Consequently, "the activity of contemplation . . . will constitute perfect happiness." (*Ethics*, 1177a)

Not only inanimate objects and men but also "all associations aim at some good" (*Politics*, 1252a) in the sense that they, too, are endowed by nature with certain definite functions or ends. And since the polis is considered by Aristotle to be the most inclusive of all actual and even possible associations, the polis "will pursue this aim most, and will thus be directed to the most sovereign of all goods" (*Ibid.*), namely, the good life. This is the end which nature has assigned to human individuals and associations regardless of whether or not it corresponds to their actual choice.

Statements about a thing's function or final end also inform us about its essence and nature. "All things derive their essential character from their function and their capacity." (*Politics*, 1253a) "The 'nature' of things consists in their end or consummation, for what each thing is when its growth is completed we call the nature of that thing, whether it be a man or a horse or a family." (*Politics*, 1252b) Assertions about a thing's function, final end, essence, or nature (they all amount to the same) must be distinguished from those assertions about goals actually chosen by men. While the latter are based on observation, the former are grounded on intuition. Indeed, Aristotle holds, like Plato, that intuition is required to apprehend essential characteristics or final causes, even though he, unlike Plato, considers that essences are not separated from observable nature but are inherent in the objects as their function and purpose.

Here the question arises: What does it mean to say that things have purposes, and that men have ends independently of those they have chosen? Ordinarily, we ascribe purposes or goals only to human activities, and only when they are deliberate. That it is my purpose to vote Republican means that I have deliberately chosen this goal in preference to other available alternatives—I myself, not "nature" (even though my choice might have been determined by "natural" events, including the influence of other actors). "Man as such" does not have purposes independently of those he happens to choose, even if it should be the case that there is some goal which men do, in fact, always pursue. Purposes in this sense cannot be ascribed to nondeliberate human or instinctive animal behavior, nor to sense organs like eyes, nor to inanimate objects like knives. Nor can human associations be said to have ends other than those of their members, except in a metaphorical sense.

It is true that certain phenomena, especially biological processes, are sometimes explained by reference to their purpose or function (Aristotle uses both concepts synonymously). When we say that leaves turn toward the sun for the purpose of absorbing light or that hens sit on eggs to hatch chicks, we do not ascribe conscious intent to leaves or hens but merely explain such phenomena in terms of the function they serve. However, functional explanations can always be translated without loss of meaning into causal explanations, and no additional information is conveyed by the use of such terms as 'purpose' or 'end'. Aristotle's ascription of purposes to nature and to things in nature is an expression of a prescientific, anthropomorphic conception of natural phenomena—as if nature were a person with the will and capacity to implant purposes into stones, plants, animals, sense organs, men, and groups. And since things are not endowed with natural purposes, the question of whether purposes can be known, by intuition or otherwise, does not even arise.

4 Finally, the statement that the good life, in the sense of the contemplative life, is the chief end of men and associations can be interpreted in the normative sense that the good life is the *desirable* end which *ought* to be chosen. Not mere life or survival, as Hart claims, but the good life or intellectual pursuit is the *proper* end of human activity.

Why? Because men and societies always seek happiness? I have pointed out that they don't; and even if they did, no normative conclusion could be derived from the factual premise. Because happiness simply consists in the attainment of whatever anyone desires? Then, as we have seen, the statement that all seek happiness becomes a mere tautology, and from tautologies nothing but tautologies can be derived. Because "the active exercise of the soul's faculties" is the final end of man? This seems to be Aristotle's own answer. Once we understand man's essence, we can arrive at moral truth, since "the end, or final cause, is the best." (*Politics*, 1253a) Rational thought and action are the functions of man. "From these premises *it follows that* the Good of man is the active exercise of his soul's faculties in conformity with excellence or virtue." (*Ethics*, 1098a; italics added) Since "nothing contrary to nature is right" (*Politics*, 1325b) but everything in accordance with nature is, it follows that it is morally obligatory for men to seek happiness, not of any kind whatsoever but the perfect happiness of the contemplative life, at least to the extent to which they are capable.

Aristotle's metaethics must, then, be characterized as naturalistic, not intuitionistic. The principle that happiness of a certain kind is intrinsically desirable he considers to be objectively true, not because it is accessible to direct intuition, but because it is derivable from premises which, in turn, are true because they agree with our intuitive knowledge. The only difference between Aristotelian and, say, Spencerian naturalism is that Aristotle's moral principle is derived not from empirical but from teleological generalizations. We have seen that intuition cannot be a source of either valuational or teleological knowledge. In fact, there *is* no teleological knowledge. If so, we need not even ask the question whether moral principles can be established as derivations from teleological generalizations.

The good of man is the subject matter of the science of politics (*Ethics*, 1094b), and much of Aristotle's *Politics* is concerned with determining what kind of political society would be most conducive to making a life of intellectual pursuits possible at least for a certain group. He includes a government of laws rather than of men and the exclusion of farmers and artisans from citizenship because they lack the leisure necessary for the happiness of the contemplative life. These are instrumental value judgments, hence, factual statements which are, at least in principle, empirically testable. If the end is given, and the means have been established, we can derive what laws and policies should be enacted by applying Aristotle's practical syllogism (outlined in Book VI of his *Ethics*): A is good; B is a means to A; therefore, B ought to be done. But how do we know that A is good? How can we show that Aristotle's kind of happiness is intrinsically desirable? Aristotle himself has not provided a convincing answer.

2 / St. Thomas Aquinas and Jacques Maritain

We have already dealt with the metaethics of Aquinas in the chapter on intuitionism; we return to him here because, as indicated earlier, he also relies on naturalistic arguments in support of the natural law thesis. Aquinas, too, holds the teleological view that all things, whether animate or inanimate, have a natural tendency to realize their respective final ends. These ends are determined, however, not by impersonal nature but by a personal God.

Now each thing is inclined naturally to an operation that is suitable to it according to its form: *e.g.*, fire is inclined to give heat. Therefore, since the rational soul is the proper form of man, there is in every man a natural inclination to act according to reason; and this is to act according to virtue. (*S.T.*, I–II, Q.94, A.3)

This does not mean that all men do, in fact, always tend to act rationally and virtuously, but that to do so is man's God-given purpose. Happiness, the final end of man, is equated by Aquinas not with the contemplative life in general but with beatitude, the contemplation of God. Rational insight enables us to know the final end. Knowledge of the final end makes it possible, in turn, to know what is good and what ought to be done to realize it, since *"good is that which all things seek after."* (Q.94, A.2)

There is in man an inclination to good according to the nature of his reason, which nature is proper to him. Thus man has a natural inclination to know the truth about God, and to live in society; and in this respect, whatever pertains to this inclination belongs to the natural law: *e.g.*

to shun ignorance, to avoid offending those among whom one has to live, and other such things regarding the above inclination. (Q.94, A.2)

Thus the principles of natural law can be known in two ways: directly through rational intuitive insight, and indirectly as derivations from assertions about man's final end which, in turn, can be known intuitively. The latter, teleological, aspect of Thomistic philosophy is subject to the same criticism as Aristotle's metaethical views.

Modern Thomists like Jacques Maritain often combine Aquinas' intuitionistic and naturalistic approaches to natural law.

The only practical knowledge all men have naturally and infallibly in common is that we must do good and avoid evil. This is the preamble and the principle of natural law; it is not the law itself. Natural law is the ensemble of things to do and not to do which follow therefrom in *necessary* fashion, and *from the simple fact that man is man*, nothing else being taken into account. (1958, p. 36)

There are, again, two ways in which moral principles can be demonstrated: (1) They follow deductively ("in necessary fashion") from the first principle of natural law that good is to be done, and this principle is a matter of indubitable practical knowledge. (This argument has been criticized in Chap. 3, III, 1.) (2) "And" it follows from the "fact" that "man is man," or that "there is a human nature, and that this human nature is the same in all men." (1951, p. 85) These statements, if taken literally, do not refer to "facts" at all but are purely tautological. All objects belonging to the same class have the same "nature," i.e., have certain properties in common, namely, those which distinguish them from objects not belonging to that class. That all men have a common human nature may also be interpreted in the Aristotelian–Thomistic, teleological sense that man possesses ends which necessarily correspond to his essential constitution and which are the same for all—as all pianos, for instance, whatever their particular type and in whatever spot they may be, have as their end the production of certain attuned sounds. If they do not produce these sounds they must be tuned, or discarded as worthless. But since man is endowed with intelligence and determines his own ends, it is up to him to put himself in tune with the ends necessarily demanded by his nature. This means that there is, by the very virtue of human nature, an order or a disposition which human reason can discover and according to which the human will must act in order to attune itself to the essential and necessary ends of the human being. The unwritten law, or natural law, is nothing more than that. (*Ibid.*, p. 86; cf. above, p. 43)

Our criticisms of Aristotle and Aquinas apply even more obviously to this passage. Pianos have no end or goal; *pianists* may have as *their* end "the production of certain attuned sounds," whether Bach or rock 'n' roll; and nonpianists might use pianos, even well-tuned ones, as billiard tables. Man, indeed, "*determines* his own ends"—*varying* ends. Consequently, it cannot also be the case that man "*possesses* ends"—"the *same* for all." This passage may also be interpreted in the normative sense that there is an end which all men *ought* to pursue, even though they may, in fact, choose to do otherwise. But then, what ought to be done is not derived from a factual statement but from a premise which already has the same, normative meaning as the conclusion.

3 / Related Examples

One difficulty with statements about man's final end or natural inclination is that they can always be interpreted in two different ways: either as factual assertions about the end implanted in man by nature or God, or as normative statements about the end he ought to pursue. Aristotle's work contains many other statements which are as ambiguous as his teleological affirmations because they contain terms which have both descriptive and valuational meaning. If such statements are understood in the factual sense, no normative principles can be derived from them; if they are taken as having themselves normative meaning, then they merely restate the normative conclusion in a different way.

'Prior', 'higher', 'natural' are examples of such ambiguous words. That *x* is prior to *y* may mean that *x* occurs before *y* in time, or that *y* somehow presupposes *x*, or that *x* is more valuable than *y*. In the following passage, 'prior' seems to assume the second meaning in the premise and the third in the conclusion. "The polis is prior in the order of nature to the family and the individual. The reason for this is that the whole is necessarily prior [in nature] to the part." (*Politics*, 1253a) This probably means that the parts presuppose the whole, and that *for this reason* the polis is more valuable than the family (even though the family emerges temporally prior to the polis). Evidently, this is not a valid argument since 'prior' has not the same meaning in the premise and in the conclusion. In the following example, both premise and conclusion seem to have valuational meaning: "Contemplation is . . . the highest form of activity (since the intellect is the highest thing in us)." (*Ethics*, 1177a) In other words, contemplation is the most valuable activity because intellect is the most valuable part of us (but Aristotle does not demonstrate that this is so).

The words 'nature' and 'natural' are used by Aristotle as synonyms of 'beneficial' and 'desirable', sometimes explicitly. Here are some examples: "It is clearly natural and beneficial to the body that it should be ruled by the soul." (*Politics*, 1254b) "It is thus clear that, just as some are by nature free, so others are by nature slaves, and for these latter the condition of slavery is both beneficial and just." (*Politics*, 1255a) "There are species in which a distinction is already marked, immediately at birth, between those of its members who are intended for being ruled and those who are intended to rule" (*Politics*, 1254a)—intended by nature. Aristotle does not explicitly draw a normative conclusion from this factual allegation but the implication is obvious: it is right that those whom nature has intended to rule should rule, and the others should obey, just as it is right for someone to be a slave if, and because, he is a slave "by nature."

The same kind of reasoning is adopted by those who claim that members of a "superior" race or people or culture or religion are morally entitled to dominate those who are by nature "inferior." But we must distinguish. That whites are naturally more intelligent than Negroes is a genuinely factual generalization which, as such, can be empirically tested—and refuted. Even if this assertion were true, it would not entail the conclusion that racial discrimination is morally legitimate without the additional *normative* premise: to each according to his innate intelligence. On the other hand, to argue that whites should occupy privileged positions because they are "superior" or of "higher intrinsic worth" than Negroes is to derive a principle of political ethics from another value judgment which, as such, cannot even in theory be subjected to any empirical test. As in the examples from Aristotle, the normative conclusion merely restates some part of the premise which is itself valuational.

The same criticism applies to the opposite doctrine, that all men *should* be treated equally because all men *are* equal. That men are equal may mean that they are, in fact, alike in certain respects; e.g., when Hobbes says that men are substantially "equal, in the faculties of the body and mind" (*Leviathan*, xiii), or when Hart speaks of the fact of approximate equality among men. From this fact alone, no normative inference can be drawn— e.g., that men should have equal rights (or that some "system of mutual forbearance and compromise" should be enacted, which is Hart's conclusion). Locke, unlike Hobbes, interprets his own statement "that all men by nature are equal" as referring not to "all sorts of equality" such as "age or virtue" but to "that equal right that every man hath to his natural freedom." (*Civil Government*, 54) That all men have equal moral rights to freedom is a normative statement to the effect that men "should also be equal one amongst another" (*Civil Government*, 4) and, hence, should be given equal rights by their respective governments. The normative conclusion merely restates the normative premise in slightly different words.

Both egalitarian and inegalitarian treatment have been justified on the grounds that they are "in agreement with nature," this latter statement being taken either in the factual or the valuational sense. However, equality or inequality of characteristics does not entail the justice, respectively, of equal or unequal distribution of benefits and burdens. There is surely no incompatibility in maintaining that all should be given equal rights and duties, even though they are of varying physical and mental endowments, just as it is consistent to hold that men should be treated unequally, e.g., as to taxation or remuneration or franchise, even though they are equal, e.g., with respect to basic needs.

III Based on Descriptive Definitions of Value Terms

We turn now to some examples of the more sophisticated version of naturalism in political philosophy. As explained earlier (Chap. 2, I, 1, a) this theory holds that value words and ethical terms, such as 'good' or 'desirable' or 'right' or 'moral duty', refer to "natural properties" and can be defined in purely descriptive terms. This form of naturalism has, therefore, also been called the *definist theory*. According to this view, a normative principle can be derived not from a factual or teleological premise alone but from a descriptive generalization together with a descriptive definition of some basic value word. Schematically, the argument may be stated as follows: (1) That x is good means that x has the property P. (2) x has the property P. (3) Hence, x is good. Here, (1) is a definition of 'good' in descriptive terms; (2) is an empirical statement; (3) is a valuational principle. According to the definist version of naturalism, too, ethics becomes essentially an empirical science. Indeed, if ethical terms are synonymous with descriptive terms, ethical principles can be translated without loss of meaning into descriptive generalizations; hence, by verifying the latter, we establish the truth of the former.

1 / Aristotle

Aristotle's philosophy illustrates both types of naturalism, and it is sometimes difficult to keep them apart. He actually uses three different arguments to establish the intrinsic desirability of happiness. (1) There is the argument which we examined in the previous section; happiness is man's ultimate goal (either in the sense that he always chooses this goal or in the sense that it is his natural and final end); therefore, the pursuit of happiness is morally right. (2) Aristotle also uses the following definist argument: "Both the multitude and persons of refinement define the good as happiness." (*Ethics*, 1095a) In other words, the value word 'good' is synonymous with the descriptive term 'happiness' ('happiness' being, in turn, "a certain activity of the soul in conformity with perfect goodness" [*Ethics*, 1102a] * although "ordinary people identify it with . . . pleasure or wealth or honor." [*Ethics*, 1095a]) Hence, if x is conducive to happiness, then x is good. (3) There is yet

---

* While 'goodness' is defined by 'happiness', 'happiness' is, in turn, defined by reference to 'goodness', which makes the whole definition circular.

another definist argument: "It has been well said that the Good is That at which all things aim" (*Ethics*, 1094a)—i.e., that which is anything's natural purpose or final end. Now, if 'x is good' is synonymous with 'there is something of which x is the final end', it follows that, if x is the final end of something, then x is good: "the end, or final cause, is the best." Happiness being the final end of man, it follows that happiness is good and that man ought to seek happiness.

Let us take, as one further example of Aristotle's definist type of naturalism, his famous statement that "the unjust is the unequal, the just is the equal." (*Ethics*, 1131a) This sentence is ambiguous, like many similar ones, since it can be interpreted either as a normative statement (it is just to act in an egalitarian way) or as a definition of the concept of justice ('justice' means the same as 'egalitarianism'). Taking it in the latter sense, we have again a descriptive definition of an ethical concept. Aristotle makes it clear that "what we are investigating, however, is the Justice which is a part of Virtue" (*Ethics*, 1130a); i.e., that just actions are a subclass of virtuous actions. While actions of any kind may be considered virtuous or evil, or morally right or wrong, 'just' or 'unjust' can be, in this sense, predicated only of actions or rules which are concerned with the distribution of benefits and burdens among several persons. While 'just' and 'unjust' are ethical concepts, 'equal' and 'unequal' are descriptive terms. A rule is egalitarian when equal shares are awarded to equals, and inegalitarian "when equals possess or are allotted unequal shares, or persons not equal equal shares." (*Ethics*, 1131a) That two persons are equal means to Aristotle that they are of equal merit or desert. Whether two shares are equal or unequal can, no doubt, be empirically determined. Whether two persons are of equal or unequal merit can, according to Aristotle, also be objectively ascertained. He considered, therefore, "proportionate equality on the basis of desert" (*Politics*, 1317b) to be a descriptive concept. Now, if a just distribution means the same as an egalitarian distribution—i.e., "one in which the relative values of the things given correspond to those of the persons receiving" (*Politics*, 1280a)—then, by showing that a rule of distribution does satisfy this condition, we have *demonstrated* that the rule is just, and that "justice in distributions must be based on desert of some sort." (*Ethics*, 1131a) On the other hand, to distribute equal shares to all, regardless of their differences in merit, is then demonstrably unjust.*

Unlike the simpler form of naturalism, the argument of definist theories cannot be criticized on purely logical grounds. If goodness is the same thing as happiness, it follows that whatever state of affairs promotes happiness is good. But the question arises: Is 'goodness' synonymous with 'happiness' or with any other decriptive term? There is the preliminary question: Can definitions be said to be either true or false?

Definitions are of three kinds. *Descriptive* definitions report what meaning is actually being attached to a given expression by those who use it. For example, 'turn on' means the same as 'excite' in the language of present-day American teenagers. A descriptive definition is true if it accurately reports the established meaning of the term to be defined.† *Stipulative* definitions "serve to introduce an expression that is to be used in some specific sense in the context of a discussion, a theory, and the like." (Hempel, 1966, p. 86) For example, Robert Dahl stipulates that "we shall use as interchangeable the terms 'popular government' and 'polyarchy' (rule by the

---

* In his *Ethics*, Aristotle defines equality in the sense of egalitarian rule—the awarding of equal shares to persons of equal merit; in his *Politics*, he distinguishes two kinds of equality: "proportional equality on the basis of desert," and arithmetical or numerical equality, i.e., equal shares to all. The latter is "the democratic conception of justice." (*Politics*, 1317a)

† The definition of 'turn on' does fulfill this condition, if the testimony of my three teenage children can be taken as evidence.

many)." (Dahl, p. 73) Such a stipulative definition cannot be true or false since it is an author's arbitrary proposal to introduce a new linguistic sign ('polyarchy') and to attach to it a certain meaning ('popular government'). *Explicative* definitions are given of expressions which are already in use in everyday or even scientific language. An explicative definition "aims at giving those expressions a new and precisely determined meaning, so as to render them more suitable for clear and rigorous discourse on the subject matter at hand." (Hempel, 1952, p. 11) For example, Dahl defines 'popular government' to refer to political systems "in which power over state officials is widely, though by no means equally, shared." (Dahl, p. 73) An explicative definition, while not, strictly speaking, either true or false, "may be adjudged more or less adequate according to the extent to which it attains its objectives." (Hempel, 1952, p. 12)

Definitions of words such as 'good' are of course intended to be explicatory. So the question is: Is it adequate to define the value term 'good' by a descriptive term such as 'happiness'? If this definition were adequate, it would be self-contradictory to maintain that something which does not contribute to happiness is good, or that something which does is bad. Now, it cannot be denied that there are people who consider certain states of affairs either good or bad, independently of whether or not they are conducive to happiness (either in Aristotle's sense or in some other meaning of the term). We may disagree with their attitudes, but we cannot criticize them as self-contradictory. Similarly, there is no inconsistency in maintaining that it is just to institute universal suffrage, i.e., to give each citizen one vote, rather than to allot voting rights according to "desert." A rule of distribution may also be considered just even though it is not egalitarian in either the proportional or the arithmetic sense. For example, someone who does not hold that whites are of greater "merit" than Negroes is bound to characterize racial discrimination inegalitarian, both arithmetically and proportionally; he may, nevertheless, consider it just to give Negroes inferior status.

Whenever the concept of goodness or rightness is defined in terms of some property, it is possible, without self-contradiction, to affirm that something does have that property, and to deny that it is good or right.

2 / Jeremy Bentham and John Stuart Mill

Definist arguments occur in both Jeremy Bentham's *Principles of Morals and Legislation* and John Stuart Mill's *Utilitarianism*. We shall, therefore, examine these two most famous expositions of classical utilitarianism together, emphasizing their similarities and ignoring, for our purposes, most of their differences.

The term 'utilitarianism' has been used rather loosely to designate various ethical doctrines which can be held independently, although it so happens that Bentham and Mill adhered to all of them. (1) In its broadest sense, utilitarianism comprises all consequence theories of ethics—those which hold that the rightness or moral worth of any action depends on the overall goodness of its consequences (see Chap. 1, II). (2) Bentham and Mill adopted happiness as the criterion of goodness, as did Aristotle. Utilitarianism, in this narrower sense, refers to that principle which states that "the greatest happiness of all those whose interest is in question, as being the right and proper, and only right and proper and universally desirable, end of human action." (*Principles*, i, fn. 1) "The creed which accepts as the foundation of morals *utility*, or the *greatest happiness principle*, holds that actions are right in proportion as they tend to promote happiness, wrong as they tend to produce the reverse of happiness." (*Utilitarianism*, ii) (3) Unlike Aristotle, Bentham and Mill used 'happiness' as a synonym for 'pleasure'. "By 'happiness' is intended pleasure, and the absence of pain; by 'unhappiness', pain, and the privation of pleasure." (*Ibid.*; see also *Principles*, i) Since happiness is intrinsically good and happiness is the same as pleasure, it follows "that pleasure, and freedom from pain, are the only things desirable as ends." (*Utilitarianism*, ii) Utilitarianism is here narrowed down to ethical hedonism. (4) Whose pleasure or happiness ought to be promoted?—"not the agent's own happiness, but that of all concerned" (*Ibid.*); in other words, "the greatest happiness of all those whose interest is in question," or the greatest happiness of the greatest number, or the greatest possible general happiness. This is the answer given by utilitarianism in the most specific sense of universalistic (as opposed to egoistic) ethical hedonism. Ideally, the principle of utility refers to the happiness or welfare "secured to all mankind." (*Ibid.*) Practically, it means that every actor ought to maximize the utility of all those affected by his action, and these may be many or few.*

Applied to the area of politics, utilitarianism, in this sense, holds that

the happiness of the individuals of whom a community is composed—that is, their pleasures and their security—is the end and the sole end which the legislator ought to have in view. (*Principles*, iii)

According to Bentham, the main function of the legislator is, therefore, to enact those, and only those, penal sanctions which are indispensable for the sole purpose of deterring as many persons as possible from acting in a way detrimental to the general welfare. To bring about "the greatest amount of happiness altogether" (*Utilitarianism*, ii), it is necessary not only to take into ac-

* The utilitarians did not distinguish explicitly between (general) happiness and good and interest and welfare, and I have not attempted to draw any distinctions here.

count the interests "of all concerned" but also to consider them equally. "Bentham's dictum, 'everybody to
count for one, nobody for more than one', might be
written under the principle of utility as an explanatory
commentary." (*Utilitarianism*, v) Maximization of total utility implies equalization of utility.

Classical utilitarianism might seem, at first glance, so
eminently plausible or even "self-evident" as to stand in
need of no further justification—until we specify some
of the ethical principles which are excluded by this doctrine. Utilitarianism in the sense of consequence theory
implies, for example, that "the motive has nothing to
do with the morality of the action" (*Utilitarianism*
ii),* and that self-sacrifice is not morally admirable unless it leads to desirable consequences. Or take such
fundamental principles of political ethics as equal
rights, or opportunities, or welfare; to each according to
his merit, or ability, or need; the retributive theory of
punishment (that sufferings imposed should be proportionate to the moral gravity of the offense). These are
nonutilitarian criteria, unless they are adopted in view
of their consequences rather than because of their intrinsic desirability.

Utilitarians, in the larger sense, need not be hedonists. In other words, consequence theories may adopt
other criteria of goodness than happiness (either in the
sense of pleasure or in some other meaning); e.g., making citizens virtuous rather than happy, or attaining and
preserving national independence even at the expense
of the citizen's well-being. Furthermore, among those
who assign the highest value to the maximization of
utility in a given society, some hold, contrary to Bentham and Mill, that this goal is not always compatible
with equality of welfare (and rightly so, I believe)
They may then value some *egalitarian* principle of dis

---

* "Though much with the worth of the agent"—so the passage
continues. Thus, Mill distinguishes between the moral rightness
of an action and the moral praiseworthiness of the actor.

tribution more highly than the realization of the *maximum* possible amount of welfare. Then there are the elitists, who desire happiness or welfare for a particular group only, either because they are indifferent to the well-being of other groups, or because they believe that privileges for a minority will actually maximize total welfare in the community.

Utilitarianism in each of its meanings is then an *ethical* theory. However, the term has also been used, very misleadingly, to refer to the *metaethical* theory that 'good' means pleasure or happiness. Again, it so happens that there are passages in Bentham and Mill reflecting this particular version of naturalism which we shall discuss in a moment. Yet the ethics of utilitarianism is, of course, compatible with the metaethics of intuitionism and value-noncognitivism as well. We shall see later that Mill himself, in one of his writings, came close to siding with noncognitivism.

Both authors affirm the factual theory of psychological hedonism as well as the normative theory of ethical hedonism. The first sentences of Bentham's *Principles* read:

Nature has placed mankind under the governance of two sovereign masters, *pain* and *pleasure*. It is for them alone to point out what we ought to do, as well as to determine what we shall do. On the one hand the standard of right and wrong, on the other the chain of causes and effects, are fastened to their throne. (i)

Similarly, Mill holds both "that there is in reality nothing desired except happiness," and "that happiness is desirable, and the only thing desirable, as an end." (*Utilitarianism*, iv) But they do not argue simply that pleasure or happiness is intrinsically desirable *because* it is desired as an end. Rather, they adopt the definist theory of naturalism. Thus, Bentham states:

Now, pleasure is in *itself* a good—nay even, setting aside immunity from pain, the only good; pain is in itself an evil—and, indeed, without exception, the only evil; or else the words good and evil have no meaning. (*Principles*, x)

Of an action that is conformable to the principle of utility, one may always say either that it is one that ought to be done, or at least that it is not one that ought not to be done. One may say also that it is right it should be done. . . . When thus interpreted, the words *ought*, and *right* and *wrong*, and others of that stamp, have a meaning: when otherwise, they have none. (*Principles*, i)

In other words: the only correct meaning of 'good' is pleasure, and the only correct meaning of 'ought' and 'right' is conformity with the principle of utility. Hence, from the fact that some state of affairs x affords pleasure, we can infer that x is good. Similarly, if action x conforms to the principle of utility, it follows that x ought to be done and that it is right to do x. And so, the principles of morals and legislation are based on empirically verifiable statements about conduciveness to happiness.

Bentham's theory is subject to the same criticism as Aristotle's. It is neither meaningless nor self-contradictory to consider it wrong to promote the greatest happiness of the greatest number, or to value some pleasurable state of affairs negatively. Mill's argument is somewhat more involved:

The only proof capable of being given that an object is visible, is that people actually see it. . . . In like manner, I apprehend, the sole evidence it is possible to produce that anything is desirable, is that people do actually desire it. . . . No reason can be given why the general happiness is desirable except that each person, so far as he believes it to be attainable, desires his own happiness. This, however, being a fact, we have not only all the proof which the case admits of, but all which it is possible to require, that happiness is a good: that each person's happiness is a good to that person, and the general happiness, therefore, is a good to the aggregate of all persons. (*Utilitarianism*, iv)

This passage may be summarized as follows: (1) One's own happiness is desired by ("is good to") each (and nothing else is ever desired for its own sake). (2) "Therefore," the general happiness is desired by all. (3) '*x* is desirable' means the same as '*x* is desired'.* (4) Therefore, the general happiness is desirable and good (and nothing else is ever desirable or good in itself).

Each of these assertions is open to criticism. (1) The factual theories of both psychological egoism (all desire to satisfy only their own interest) and psychological hedonism (all desire only pleasure for its own sake) have been successfully refuted,† but we need not be concerned with this issue here. (2) Indeed, even if egoistic psychological hedonism were true, it would not follow that universalistic psychological hedonism is true. If everybody always desires his own pleasure or happiness or welfare, then he does not also desire the welfare of others, let alone of all others, unless these goals are compatible. This both Bentham and Mill did believe to be the case, maintaining that it is always to one's own advantage to promote the general interest, or at least to be under a government which does. Yet, it is one of the basic facts of politics that the interest of any one person or group may conflict with that of others, and with the general interest as well (assuming that this latter objective could be objectively determined).‡ (3) While '*x* is visible' is synonymous with '*x can* be seen' (rather than with '*x* is being seen'), '*x* is desirable' means, according to well-established usage, not that *x is* being desired or

* It is at least possible to interpret Mill this way, even though he merely states that actual desire of something is "evidence" for its desirability.

† See Frankena, pp. 19–20, 67 ff.; Brandt, 1959, pp. 307 ff.

‡ In fact, it is impossible to make generalizations to the effect that there is some single goal which all men always pursue, be it pleasure or some other utilitarian, or nonutilitarian, end, be it their own advantage or the interest of some others or of all members in a given society, themselves included.

can be desired, but that x *ought* to be desired; hence, that x is *good*. While 'visible' is a descriptive term, 'desirable' is an evaluative word. Not only is it sensible to say: "x is desired, but it is not desirable"; more than that: nobody would argue that x ought to be desired because there is someone who desires x. (4) The principle of utility or universalistic ethical hedonism is derived by Mill from egoistic psychological hedonism (1), with the help of (2) and (3). We have seen that (1) and (3) are false and that (2) does not follow from (1); hence, the argument does not establish the truth of (4) as a conclusion. Moreover, even if (2) were true, i.e., even if all men were in fact benevolent (rather than egoistic) hedonists, it still would not follow that all men *ought* to desire the general happiness.

Both Bentham and Mill hold that a state of affairs x is intrinsically better than y if and only if x is more pleasurable than y; but they differ as to the meaning of statements of the type: 'x is more pleasurable than y'. To Bentham, this is an empirical assertion about the comparative quantity of pleasure generated by x and y: pleasures differ only quantitatively; the degree of intensity of a pleasure a person feels can be measured, e.g., its duration; and it is possible to compare and to measure not only how much pleasure the same person A derives from two alternative states of affairs but also how much pleasure two persons A and B derive from the same state of affairs x.

However, utilitarianism is not tied to Bentham's theory of the calculus of pleasure, which has been justly criticized. According to Mill, pleasures differ in quality as well as quantitatively; hence, it is possible that the pleasure afforded by state of affairs x is superior in quality to that of y, even though the latter pleasure may be quantitatively greater, e.g., as to duration. "It is quite compatible with the principle of utility to recognize the fact, that some *kinds* of pleasure are more desirable and more valuable than others." (*Utilitarianism*, ii) And pleasure of kind x is more valuable than pleasure of kind y if x is qualitatively superior to y, even though y may be quantitatively the greater pleasure. "It is better to be a human being dissatisfied than a pig satisfied" (*Ibid.*); a smaller quantity of a qualitatively higher pleasure is preferable to a greater quantity of a lower pleasure.

Now, the statement that x is a qualitatively higher kind of pleasure than y is not an empirical assertion but a value judgment (just like the statement that x is more desirable or valuable than y). The question then arises whether a value judgment of this type can be objectively justified. Mill answers affirmatively: "The test of quality, and the rule for measuring it against quantity, [is] the preference felt by those who in their opportunities of experience . . . are best furnished with the means of comparison." (*Ibid.*) That pleasure x is of a higher quality than pleasure y means, then, that x is preferred to y by competent judges who have experienced both x and y.* Consequently, if x is preferred by competent judges, then x is the higher pleasure, then x is more desirable and valuable and ought to be brought about. "On a question which is the best worth having of two pleasures, . . . the judgment of those who are qualified by knowledge of both, or, if they differ, that of the majority among them, must be admitted as final." (*Ibid.*) It must be—provided we admit Mill's definition of 'higher pleasure'. But again, it is not self-contradictory to deny that x is a higher pleasure than y, even though x is preferred to y by the majority of qualified judges.† Mill has not succeeded in justifying the moral principle that one should make those pleasures

---

* It is not certain, however, whether the last quoted statement is to be interpreted as a definition of the valuational expression 'higher pleasure' in descriptive terms, or as a value judgment to the effect that a state of affairs which is preferred by qualified judges is a superior kind of pleasure.

† Nor has Mill demonstrated that a pleasure which is, in this sense, higher is necessarily the more desirable.

which are preferred by most competent experts avail
able to the greatest possible number.

3 / Subjectivism

Certain naturalists define valuational or ethical con
cepts by reference to subjective preferences (see Chap
2, I, 1, a). Mill's definition of 'higher pleasures' involv
ing 'preferences felt by the majority of qualified judges
is an example of this type of definist theory, which ha
been labeled subjectivism. This term is rather mislead
ing since the theory holds that if certain persons have a
positive subjective feeling about some state of affairs
then that state of affairs is *objectively* desirable. So
called subjectivism belongs then to the metaethics o
cognitivism, and must be distinguished from the non
cognitivist view that value judgments are mere *expres
sions* of preferences.

The rise of democratic theory and practice has beer
associated not only with the normative view that gov
ernmental decisions should implement majority prefer
ences but also with the subjectivist metaethical theory
that this normative principle is true because 'x is intrin
sically desirable' is synonymous with 'x is preferred by
the majority'. What is good and right may vary from
one time and society to another according to the vary
ing valuational attitudes of the majority. At any given
time and place, however, objective goodness and right
ness correspond to the prevailing moral standards. This
particular naturalistic theory must be distinguished no
only from noncognitivism but from intuitionism a
well. The claim is not that values and norms can be
directly apprehended by moral insight, and that as a
matter of fact they are correctly intuited by all except a
minority (this seems to be Rousseau's view; see Chap
3, I, 2). The argument is rather: that some alternative is
preferred by most means that this policy is objectively
desirable. Affirmations about prevailing preferences and

moral convictions of a given group at a given time are empirical statements which can be tested by such devices as public opinion polls.

It is true that, given the definition: 'x is desirable = x is generally preferred', and given the fact that the majority approves of x, it follows that x is desirable and ought to be realized. But again, the proposed definition is surely unacceptable. Someone who says that racial discrimination is wrong is surely not just making a factual assertion about someone's valuations, whether his own or someone else's or the majority's. Furthermore, someone who says that racial discrimination is wrong even though his community as a whole tends to consider it right is surely not contradicting himself, as he would if wrongness *meant* the same as public disapproval.

This particular definist position may be illustrated by another passage from the same book by Carl Friedrich which has already provided examples for intuitionism as well as naturalism in its simpler form.

An action may be said to be just, and hence likewise a rule, judgment or a decision, when it involves a comparative valuation of the persons affected by the action, and when that comparison accords with the values and beliefs of the political community. (Friedrich, p. 251)

The normative concept of a just rule is defined here, as in Aristotle, by reference to the comparative worth of those to whom the rule applies. However, a person's relative worth is to be determined not by some alleged objective standard but by the assessment of the majority. It would follow that racial discrimination is just in a community in which race is generally considered a determining factor of a person's comparative worth.

According to another subjectivist theory, 'x is morally right' means the same as 'x is, or would be, approved by any rational actor'. Here are two examples:

What people *ought to* desire is what they *would* desire i
they were enlightened and knew both what they reall
wanted and what natural means would bring it about. Mo
rality is thus wisdom applied to the conduct of life, and
yields rules which we would follow if we thought out all the
implications of our choices and knew in advance their con
sequences. (Cohen and Nagel, p. 366)

If a clear definition of rationality could be found, then w
might say that, "X ought to do A" means that "X would d
A if his behavior were rational." (Churchman, p. 219)

It has been pointed out (Chap. 2, II, 1) that actin
rationally is not the same as acting morally, that
course of action can be said to be rational only wit
respect to some given valuational standard, and that on
may act or fail to act rationally with respect to any suc
standard.* Making rational choices on the basis of
given, e.g., the utilitarian, standard may, of course, b
adopted as a *normative* principle. Presumably, the au
thor did not mean to imply that if the Nazis went abou
rationally to exterminate the Jews (as they in fact did
then they ought to have done so and their behavior wa
right.

A variation of this view is the so-called ideal observe
theory, the most widely accepted form of naturalism a
the present time. Here the expression: 'x is intrinsicall
right' is equated with: 'x would be approved by anyon
who has the disposition to be rational, impartial, un
emotional, and normal'. The underlying assumption
that there would be no ethical disagreement amon
"ideal observers" who know all the relevant facts, wh
are not personally involved in the issue (or who are abl
to disregard their personal interests), who apply co
rectly the rules of inductive and deductive reasonin
etc. For example,

---

* The author of the last-quoted passage is aware of this distin
tion; see Churchman, p. 233.

normal people who are *fully aware* of what is involved would make the judgment "Democracy is good." In our view, this would express the inescapable imperative of practical reason. (Pennock, p. 53; italics added)

Accordingly,

we need not, in our ethical and value judgments, give up the claim that they are objectively valid in the sense that they will be sustained by a review by all those who are free, clear-headed, fully informed, and who take the point of view in question. (Frankena, 1963, pp. 93–94)

This theory has the advantage of being immune to the objection against definism in general and subjectivism in particular since it defines the concept of goodness in terms not of actual approval by actual people but of how some ideal observer would feel if he existed. The ideal observer theory must be criticized on other grounds, however. First of all, it just is not true that

certain attitudes will be inevitable in persons whose cognitive orientations are sound, whose past lives have included normal interactions with a family and other persons, and who are free from distortions produced by fear and anxiety. (Brandt, 1963, p. 8)

The belief that there are such common attitudes among all "normal" people everywhere is perhaps due to the circumstance that the United States and England happen to be by and large free from fundamental ideological cleavages at the present time. This is already less true of Western Europe and not at all when we consider the whole world. Different persons, especially from different countries and continents, may agree on all the relevant facts concerning race, birth control, civil disobedience, communism, revolution, nuclear armaments, etc., have "normal interactions with a family," and fulfill all the other requirements of the ideal observer, and yet have diametrically opposed attitudes as to what is intrinsically desirable in connection with such issues.

There is a further criticism. We mentioned earlier (Chap. 1, II) the fallacy of defining descriptive concepts by using valuational terms, e.g., 'democracy' by using 'the good society in operation'. We have also seen that it is just as misleading to define value words with the help of descriptive terms, e.g., 'good' with 'happiness', or 'just' with 'equal', or 'desirable' with 'preferred by . . .'. Some naturalists go even further and provide definitions for valuational concepts which in turn include value words. This criticism applies to Aristotle's circular definition: 'goodness = happiness = activity in conformity with *goodness*', and also to his equation: 'just distribution = giving equal shares to persons of equal *desert*'.

The ideal observer theory must be challenged on these same grounds. True, whether a person is well informed, disinterested, and disposed to think and act rationally can in principle be objectively determined not so, however, whether someone is "normal," "sound," "free," "clear-headed." These are words with strong laudatory connotations which overshadow whatever descriptive meanings they may have. We tend to bestow such characteristics on those, and only those who happen to agree with us, be it on the factual or the normative level. Thus, Professor Brandt seems to equate a person "in a normal frame of mind" with a person "of good will" and with "a person of a normal degree of altruism or concern with the welfare of other persons." (1963, pp. 5, 6) A person who approves of the political system of Nazi Germany or of South Africa or even of Herbert Spencer would then be abnormal. Yet these are *moral* principles of politics, however immoral they may be judged by those committed to the welfare of all. Such ethical systems can be, and have been adopted in good faith by "normal" people and taken as the basis of rational behavior (unless they are them-

elves internally inconsistent, as the Nazi ideology may
well be). They cannot be shown to be objectively false
by pointing out that they have been rejected by those
who are, *by mere definition*, normal, sound, free, and of
good will.

The ideal observer theory purports to define the morally right in contradistinction to the morally wrong, not
the moral in contrast to the nonmoral. Other contemporary philosophers tend to use the concept of morals
itself to cover only one specific system of morality, the
one which happens to be generally professed (if not always practiced) in contemporary Western civilization.
According to this position,

certain material principle or goal is regarded as built into
the definition of terms like "moral" and "morality" if these
are used in anything like their normal sense. . . . This
material condition . . . must reflect a concern for others
or a consideration of social cohesiveness and the common
good. (Frankena, 1965, pp. 11, 9)

This is precisely the substantive moral principle which
built into Baier's characterization of "the moral point
of view." (Cf. Frankena, *loc. cit.*, for other examples of
his position which is not his own.) These authors provide, not an explicative, but a persuasive definition of
what is moral, to the exclusion, not of what is nonmoral, but of what is—to them—immoral. Metaethical
issues cannot be resolved by definitional fiat.

5

Noncognitivism as
a Political Philosophy

Our examination of intuitionism and naturalism in
their application to political ethics has led us to criticize
these two schools of value-cognitivism from a noncognitivist point of view. We shall now deal more explicitly
with this latter type of moral philosophy. Noncognitivism as a systematic theory has been worked out mainly
by philosophers who have had at most an incidental interest in political problems.* Conversely, many political
writers not primarily interested in philosophy have
adopted the conclusions of noncognitivist metaethics
and adapted them to their own purposes. This is true
especially of present-day political scientists engaged in
empirical research.

* Hobbes is an exception, but he is a borderline case, as we shall
see in a moment. Machiavelli, too, comes to mind, but he did not
work out a systematic metaethical theory.

I Refutation of Cognitivism

1 / Thomas Hobbes

Hobbes' writings no doubt contain many passages which, taken by themselves, would classify him as an exponent of the natural law thesis in particular and of value-cognitivism in general, both of the intuitionistic and the naturalistic variety. Yet these cognitivist views are implicitly and even explicitly contradicted at other places, and it is often (but not always) possible to reinterpret the former statements so that they become compatible with the latter. There are also positive affirmations of the noncognitivist position—perhaps the first to be made by a major political thinker—and this is the reason why I discuss Hobbes' metaethics at this point. We need not, for our purposes, take part in the ongoing debate as to which of the two metaethical views is preponderant in Hobbes' philosophy.

The cognitivist aspect of Hobbes' system is brought out in statements such as: "A *law of nature, lex naturalis,* is a precept or general rule, found out by reason, by which a man is forbidden to do that which is destructive of his life." (*Leviathan*, xiv) In the same context, Hobbes speaks of the "fundamental law of nature, by which men are commanded to endeavor peace." (*Ibid.*) Similarly, "justice, that is to say, performance of covenant, and giving to every man his own, is a dictate of the law of nature." (*Leviathan*, xxvi) Precepts of natural law are not only "found out by reason"; they are also manifestations of divine revelation, "for natural laws being eternal, and universal, are all divine." (*Ibid.*) Aquinas would have subscribed to each of these views: There are general moral "precepts" of the "law of nature" which "command" all men, e.g., to give to each his due, and "forbid" them to do otherwise, and these can be known through reason and revelation.

The latter source must be excluded, however, when we consider Hobbes' philosophy as a whole. Hobbes holds reason to be the only source of knowledge, to the exclusion of sense experience, and of religious experience as well. We cannot call knowledge in the philosophical sense

that which any man knows by supernatural revelation; because it is not acquired by reasoning: Nor that which is gotten by reasoning from the authority of books; because it is not . . . knowledge but faith. (*Leviathan*, xlvi)

These considerations apply also to the knowledge of moral principles. If A is convinced that God has revealed to him some moral law and B has not received such a revelation, then—so Hobbes argues—there is no objective criterion by which B can determine whether A's conviction is warranted. "God may command a man by a supernatural way, to deliver laws to other men. But . . . *how can a man without supernatural revelation be assured of the revelation received by the declarer?*" (*Leviathan*, xxvi) By miracles which the declarer performs, or by the sanctity of his life, or by the "felicity of his actions"?

Miracles are marvellous works: but that which is marvellous to one, may not be so to another. Sanctity may be feigned; and the visible felicities of this world, are most often the work of God by natural, and ordinary causes. And therefore no man can infallibly know by natural reason that another has had a supernatural revelation of God's will. (*Ibid.*)

Can the truth of certain moral principles be known *directly* by infallible natural reason? This, too, is sometimes denied by Hobbes.

This common measure [of what is to be called right, what good, what virtue . . .], some say, is right reason: with whom I should consent, if there were any such thing to be ound or known *in rerum natura*. But commonly they that call for right reason to decide any controversy, do mean their own. (*Elements of Law*, II, x, 8)

It is the *rationality*, not the morality, of certain actions which, according to Hobbes, right reason enables us to ascertain. Now, it is a fact that "all men agree on this, that peace is good, and therefore also the way, or means of peace . . . are good." (*Leviathan*, xv) To live in peace and security is the one goal which all of us have in common, and reason enables us to find out the means which will best attain it. "These dictates of reason . . . are but conclusions, or theorems concerning what conduceth to the conservation and defence of themselves" (*Ibid.*), i.e., what actions are conducive to man's self-preservation.

It is at least possible to interpret Hobbes' concept of natural law as referring to the rules of rational choice in view of the ultimate goal of individual self-preservation. "For the laws of nature . . . are not properly laws, but qualities that dispose men to peace and obedience." (*Leviathan*, xxvi)

Therefore the law of nature . . . is the dictate of right reason, conversant about those things which are either to be done or omitted *for the constant preservation of life* and members, as much as in us lies. (*De Cive*, ii, 1; italics added)*

Hobbes' laws of nature would then turn out to be not principles of political *ethics* which are *true* but princi-

---

* Cf. also the following passage:

By right reason . . . I understand not, as many do, an infallible faculty, but the act of reasoning, that is, the peculiar and true ratiocination of every man concerning those actions of his which may either redound to the damage or benefit of his neighbours. . . . I call it true, that is, concluding from true principles rightly framed, because that the whole breach of the laws of nature consists in the false reasoning, or rather folly of those men who see not those duties they are necessarily to perform towards others *in order to* their own conservation. (*Ibid.*, fn.; italics added)

ples of political *action* which are *rational*. Such a concept of natural law has nothing to do with the natural
law philosophy. As we have pointed out (Chap. 2, I, 3,
a), judgments of rationality constitute extrinsic value
judgments, which both cognitivists and noncognitivists
consider to be in principle cognitively either true or false.
Any noncognitivist could therefore agree with Hobbes'
analysis, except to point out that judgments of rationality involve empirical considerations as well as deductive
reasoning.

The difference between the natural law thesis and
Hobbes' so-called laws of nature becomes even more
manifest when we look at their content. Hobbes starts
from the empirical assumption that every man is basically self-interested, concerned above all with his own
preservation, and about as strong as any of his fellow
men. Given these circumstances, it becomes rational to
find a way out of the state of nature, which is a state of
war of all against all, where life is "solitary, poor, nasty,
brutish, and short." (*Leviathan*, xiii) Hence, "the precepts, by which men are guided to avoid that condition
[of war], are the laws of nature" (*Leviathan*, xxxi) in
the sense of rules of rationality. "And consequently it is
a precept, or general rule of reason, *that every man
ought to endeavour peace*, as far as he has hope of ob-
taining it." (*Leviathan*, xiv) Absolute government is, to
Hobbes, the only alternative to anarchy; consequently
there is only one road to civil peace: All must mutually
agree to set up a political authority and to submit to
whatever positive laws the sovereign might enact.* The
duty to obey all positive laws is entailed by the further
law of nature, "*that men perform their covenants
made*." (*Leviathan*, xv)

---

* There are, however, certain rights, e.g., that of self-defense,
"which no man can be understood by any words, or other signs,
to have abandoned, or transferred . . . because he cannot be
understood to aim thereby, at any good to himself." (*Leviathan*,
xiv)

By the virtue of the natural law which forbids breach of covenant, the law of nature commands us to keep all the civil laws. For where we are tied to obedience, before we know what will be commanded us, there we are universally tied to obey in all things. Whence it follows, that no civil law whatsoever, which tends not to a reproach of the Deity . . can possibly be against the law of nature. For though the law of nature forbid theft, adultery, &c, yet if the civil law command us to invade anything, that invasion is not theft, adultery, &c. (*De Cive*, xiv, 10)

Whereas proponents of the natural law thesis specify certain *substantive* principles which legislators are *morally* bound to translate into positive law and citizens are morally obliged to obey (sometimes in preference to conflicting positive law), Hobbes' so-called laws of nature are purely *formal* and *nonmoral*. Citizens ought to comply with whatever laws are enacted by the sovereign, but this is a matter of rational behavior, not of moral duty. The legislator, on the other hand, is (with a few exceptions) free to legislate as he pleases since there are no substantive "higher laws" with which his positive enactments could possibly conflict.

This interpretation of Hobbes' concept of natural law is corroborated by his explicit affirmation of the metaethics of noncognitivism.

But whatsoever is the object of any man's appetite or desire, that is it which he for his part calleth *good*; and the object of his hate and aversion, *evil*; and of his contempt, *vile* and *inconsiderable*. For these words of good, evil, and contemptible, are ever used with relation to the person that useth them: there being nothing simply and absolutely so; nor any common rule of good and evil, to be taken from the nature of the objects themselves. (*Leviathan*, vi)

Nothing is "simply and absolutely" either good or evil because these words do not designate inherent properties of things or states of affairs but serve to express the speaker's attitude of approval or disapproval. Conse-

quently, no objective principles of good and evil can be
derived "from the nature of the objects themselves."

Good and *evil* are names that signify our appetites and
aversions; which in different tempers, customs, and doc
trines of men, are different . . . . And therefore so long
as a man is in the condition of mere nature, which is a
condition of war, his private appetite is the measure of
good and evil. (*Leviathan*, xv)

Again, value judgments are mere expressions of the
speaker's "appetites and aversions," and thus cannot
claim to have intersubjective validity in the way descrip
tive statements are true or false, since there are no ob
jective measures of good and evil.* Since men differ in
their preferences, the same thing may be considered de
sirable by some and undesirable by others, and the lack
of an objective criterion is one of the reasons why the
state of nature is a state of war. Hobbes goes even fur
ther than contemporary noncognitivists: since nothing
is objectively either good or evil, right or wrong, just or
unjust, these words are meaningless, and hence of no
use unless there is some "civil society."

To this war of every man against every man, this also is
consequent: *that nothing can be unjust*. The notions of
right and wrong, justice and injustice, have there no place.
Where there is no common power, there is no law; where
no law, no injustice. (*Leviathan*, xiii)

The only way out of the moral as well as social chaos of
the state of nature is to set up a commonwealth where
conflicts of value and of interest are settled authorita
tively, and where private moral attitudes are superseded
by official legal rules. Under civil government, "th

---

* This passage may, however, be interpreted in the sense that
A's utterance '*x* is good' *means* ("signifies") that A approves of
x. Hobbes evidently was not aware of the distinction between the
subjectivist (cognitivist) and the emotive (noncognitivist) theor
(See Chap. 2, I, 2)

measure of good and evil actions, is the civil law." (*Leviathan*, xxix) "Laws are the rules of just, and unjust; nothing being reputed unjust, that is not contrary to some law." (*Leviathan*, xxvi) "Legitimate kings therefore make the things they command just, by commanding them, and those which they forbid, unjust, by forbidding them." (*De Cive*, xii, 1)

But here, it might be argued, Hobbes espouses a definist type of *naturalism*, construing 'action A is just or right or good' as synonymous with: 'action A is commanded or permitted by positive law', and an action as unjust if and only if it is illegal, so that it is morally right to obey the law and wrong to act illegally. Again, Hobbes' system as a whole suggests another possible interpretation: It is mistaken to affirm or to deny that such and such actions are *morally* right or just or good because these words do not designate properties which actions or states of affairs may either have or lack but "signify our appetites and aversions" concerning such actions or states of affairs. An expression such as: 'action x is unjust' cannot therefore be synonymous with the meaningful affirmation that x is prohibited by some system of positive law. There are only two kinds of normative utterances, expressions of subjective likes and dislikes and positive legal commands and prohibitions. That citizens ought to comply with all the laws enacted by the sovereign, regardless of whether or not they approve of them, is not a matter of moral duty (there are no general ethical principles) but of legal obligation (derived from the social contract) and of rational behavior in view of the goal of civil tranquillity).

2 / David Hume

Hume's metaethics constitutes the classic rebuttal of cognitivism and defense of noncognitivism, and Hume's arguments have exercised a decisive influence on contemporary noncognitivists. We must therefore consider his philosophy, even though the political aspects of human behavior were not of primary concern to him.

To understand Hume's metaethical theory it is necessary to consider a brief summary of his epistemology. Hume distinguishes sharply between two kinds of reasoning, deductive and inductive. Through *deductive reasoning* we are able to know which "relations of ideas" are conceivable and which are inconceivable; translated into modern terminology, whether a given sentence is logically true or false.

On the other hand, whatever happens in fact could be otherwise; hence, statements of fact can always be denied without contradiction and are therefore

incapable of demonstration. Whatever *is* may *not be*. No negation of a fact can involve a contradiction. . . . That the cube root of 64 is equal to the half of 10 is a false proposition and can never be distinctly conceived. But that Caesar, or the angel Gabriel, or any being never existed may be a false proposition, but still is perfectly conceivable and implies no contradiction. (*Human Understanding* Sect. xii, Part iii)

We cannot demonstrate that Caesar lived, nor that it is lightning now, nor that lightning is always followed by thunder since it is logically possible that Caesar never existed, that it is not lightning now, or that lightning is not always followed by thunder. If the factual statement that it is lightning now is warranted, it is not so on logical grounds but because I observe this event. But what is the basis of the knowledge of causal laws? We do not observe causes, we only experience particular instances e.g., of lightning *followed* by thunder. "All events seem entirely loose and separate. One event follows another, but we never can observe any tie between them. They seem *conjoined*, but never *connected*." (*Human Understanding*, Sect. vii, Part ii) But after having experienced *frequently* that lightning and thunder are "conjoined" in time, we are inclined to make the *inductive generalization* that lightning is *always* followed by thunder, and that the former kind of event is causally "connected" with the latter. Inductive reasoning is a matter of instinct, custom, or habit. Men "acquire, by long habit, such a turn of mind that upon the appearance of the cause they immediately expect, with assurance, its usual attendant, and hardly conceive it possible that any other event could result from it." (*Ibid.*, Part i) Yet, it *is* logically possible that a different event might have occurred. The statement describing the effect is not a logical consequence of the statement describing the cause. Causal statements are never true with certainty, but only with some degree of probability, since they are based on a limited number of particular instances and may be invalidated by new evidence. We have no choice, however. Induction is "that reasoning which can alone assure us of any matter of fact or existence." (*Ibid.*, Part ii)

Hume does not admit of other sources of understanding than deductive and inductive reasoning, the former conveying knowledge which is certain but merely tautological, the latter leading to information which is factual but merely probable. Pure reasoning, without reference to sense experience, does not yield new information, let alone factual knowledge which is certain. There are no "self-evident" factual truths, and there can be no rational insight into "essences" or "final causes." *An Inquiry Concerning Human Understanding* ends with these words:

When we run over libraries, persuaded of these principles, what havoc must we make? If we take in our hand any volume—of divinity or school metaphysics, for instance—let us ask, *Does it contain any abstract reasoning concerning quantity or number?* No. *Does it contain any experimental reasoning concerning matter of fact and existence?* No. Commit it then to the flames; for it can contain nothing but sophistry and illusion. (Sect. xii, Part iii)

For the same reason that particular factual statements and general causal laws cannot be demonstrated, moral principles cannot be proven. We cannot conceive of any judgment of value or of preference the contrary of which is not also conceivable. "It is not contrary to reason to prefer the destruction of the whole world to the scratching of my finger." (*Treatise*, II, Part III, 3) "The rules of morality, therefore, are not conclusions of our reason." (*Treatise*, III, Part I, 1) Similarly, "the sense of justice is not founded on reason, or on the discovery of certain connections and relations of ideas which are eternal, immutable, and universally obligatory." (*Treatise*, III, Part II, 2) Here is a sweeping indictment of the rational-insight variety of intuitionism. And since Hume denies the possibility of any kind of synthetic *a priori* knowledge, there can be no moral or religious intuition of morality either.

Nor are moral judgments factually true or false, as observation statements are, because goodness or badness, beauty or ugliness, virtue or vice are not observable qualities of objects or actions.

Take any action allowed to be vicious—wilful murder, for instance. Examine it in all lights, and see if you can find that matter of fact or real existence which you call *vice*. In whichever way you take it, you find only certain passions, motives, volitions, and thoughts. There is no other matter of fact in the case. The vice entirely escapes you, as long as you consider the object. (*Treatise*, III, Part I, 1)

All we can observe is the sequence of events leading from the murderer's lifting of the gun to the death of his victim. No normative statement can be derived from a factual statement, either inductively or deductively.

In every system of morality which I have hitherto met with, I have always remarked that the author proceeds for some time in the ordinary way of reasoning, and establishes the being of a god, or makes observations concerning human affairs; when of a sudden I am surprised to find that instead of the usual copulations of propositions *is* and *is not*, I meet with no proposition that is not connected with an *ought* or an *ought not*. This change is imperceptible, but it is, however, of the last consequence. For as this *ought* or *ought not* expresses some new relation or affirmation, it is necessary that . . . a reason should be given for what seems altogether inconceivable, how this new relation can be a deduction from others which are entirely different from it. (*Ibid.*)

No reason *can* be given. Affirmations about the existence of God or about human behavior are factual statements; no normative conclusions can be drawn from them, since a conclusion cannot contain anything which is not in the premises. Here we have a refutation of the simple form of naturalism. We shall see in a moment that Hume does not subscribe to the definist theory either, even though certain passages seem to indicate that he does.

If ethical principles cannot be demonstrated like mathematical theorems, nor empirically verified like observation statements, nor deductively or inductively inferred from statements of fact, then Hume must conclude that "it is impossible, therefore, they can be pronounced either true or false." (*Ibid.*) We have seen that, according to Hume, valuational and ethical concepts do not designate objective properties, and that therefore the viciousness of the murder "entirely escapes you" if you consider the murder itself. This passage continues:

You never find it till you turn your reflection into your own breast and find a sentiment of disapprobation which arises in you towards this action. Here is a matter of fact; but it is the object of feeling, not of reason. It lies in yourself, not in the object. So that when you pronounce any action or character to be vicious, you mean nothing, but that from the constitution of your nature you have a feeling or sentiment of blame from the contemplation of it. (*Ibid.*)

Hume probably does not intend to convey the idea that when you pronounce an action vicious, you *mean* the same as that you do have a sentiment of disapprobation toward this action. This would imply that your pronouncement is *true* if indeed you have such a feeling, which would be incompatible with Hume's central thesis that moral judgments cannot be pronounced either true or false. More likely, this passage is to be interpreted, like Hobbes' similar statement, in the noncognitivist, not in the subjectivist, sense. To say that an action is vicious or morally wrong is to *express* one's sentiment of blame toward that action, with the intention of *influencing* the behavior of one's listeners.* "Morals excite passions, and produce or prevent actions." (*Ibid.*) Consequently, if someone has a moral sentiment opposed to my own,

I know not how I should address myself to such a one, or by what arguments I should endeavor to reform him. . . . But, then, I ask, if any other philosophy can afford a remedy, or if it be possible, by any system, to render all mankind virtuous, however perverse may be their natural frame of mind? (*Essays*, Part I, Essay XIII)

In other words, there is no way of demonstrating that all men ought to act in a way which meets with my own approval and which I myself would therefore call virtuous (and of persuading them to act that way). "Morality . . . is entirely relative to the sentiment or mental taste of each particular being." (*Human Understanding*, Sect. i, fn. 2)

There are passages in which Hume seems to adopt another definist theory, namely that the expression 'this action is virtuous' means that this action is approved, not just by the speaker but universally, or that

* This is the usual interpretation. See, for example, Benn and Peters, p. 41: "Hume meant, surely, that when people make moral judgments they are *expressing* approval or disapproval, not describing how they feel."

this action has pleasurable consequences for all concerned, or that this action tends to promote the general welfare. (See, for example, *Principles of Morals*, Sect. ix, Part i) It is difficult to reconcile such naturalistic views with Hume's central noncognitivist theory. It is not always clear, however, whether he means to *define* morally right or wrong actions in terms of "those universal sentiments of censure or approbation which arise from humanity or from views of general usefulness and its contrary" (*Ibid.*), or to make the *empirical generalization* that there are such universally shared sentiments. Hume does emphasize that people do, on the whole, have the same moral feelings and ultimate goals. So, while in theory "morality is relative to the moral taste of each," there are in fact "universal sentiments of censure and approbation." Yet,

it appears evident that the ultimate ends of human actions can never, in any case, be accounted for by *reason*, but recommend themselves entirely to the sentiments and affections of mankind, without any dependence on the intellectual faculties. (*Ibid.*, Appendix 1)

This is not to deny that inductive and deductive reasoning enables us to arrive at moral judgments, choices, and actions which are *rational* with respect to these universally adopted ultimate goals. Rational evaluation involves approving or disapproving of actions and their outcomes not in isolation but by virtue of certain of their general characteristics, and these relevant features must be known before giving our feelings free rein.

In moral decisions, all circumstances and relations must be previously known; and the mind, from the contemplation of the whole, feels some new impression of affection or disgust, esteem or contempt, approbation or blame. (*Ibid.*)

Here is, at least implicitly, a reference to the principle of universalizability (see Chap. 2, I, 3, a): our prefer-

ences, to be rational, must be expressed by principles
which are general (whatever their content may be), and
thus applicable to all particular circumstances which are
similar in the specified respect. Among the "relations
which must be previously known" are the causal connections between the means, the contemplated end
and its further consequences. Thus, reason

> can have an influence on our conduct only after two ways:
> either when it excites a passion by informing us of the ex-
> istence of something which is a proper object of it; or when
> it discovers the connection of causes and effects so as to
> afford us means of exerting any passion. (*Treatise*, III, Part
> I, 1)

However, "where a passion is neither founded on false
suppositions, nor chooses means insufficient for the
end, the understanding can neither justify nor condemn
it." (*Treatise*, II, Part III, 3)

In the political sphere, Hume is, like Hobbes, mainly
concerned with the empirical question why it is that
men more or less willingly live in a political society and
tend to comply even with those laws which enjoin them
to act contrary to their apparent self-interest. Hume's
answer, different from Hobbes', is that men live thus
not because they have explicitly consented to be legally
bound, nor out of fear of punishment inflicted by those
in power, but because they realize that it is in the long
range interest of each that all submit to political authority. This "general sense of common interest" develops
into a habit, like the tacit agreement of "two men who
pull the oars of a boat," or the gradual formation of
languages (*Treatise*, III, Part II, 2), or our inductive
reasoning.

> No maxim is more conformable, both to prudence and
> morals, than to submit quietly to the government which we
> find established in the country where we happen to live,
> without inquiring too curiously into its origin and first es-
> tablishment. (*Ibid.*, 10)

To submit to government is, then, a rule of prudence, i.e., of rationality in view of the preservation of peace and the protection of property which happen to constitute, according to Hume, man's ultimate political goal. It is a maxim of morals only in the instrumental sense that it indicates the means which are necessary to attain this ultimate end. The former can be justified on the basis of inductive reasoning; the latter is a matter of subjective feeling, however universal it may be.

Nothing could be further from Hume's political philosophy than the natural law thesis; and yet Hume, like Hobbes, sometimes uses the terminology of natural law.

Mankind is an inventive species; and where an invention is obvious and absolutely necessary, it may . . . be said to be natural. . . . Though the rules of justice be *artificial*, they are not *arbitrary*. Nor is the expression improper to call them *laws of nature*, if by *natural* we understand what is common to any species, or even if we confine it to mean what is inseparable from the species. (*Ibid.*, 1)

Paradoxically, Hume's "natural" laws are at the same time "artificial," since they are "invented" by men. They are "natural" merely in the sense of being necessary to social cohesion and, in fact, enacted in all societies.* There are "three fundamental laws of nature, *that of the stability of possession, of its transference by consent*, and *of the performance of promises*." (*Ibid.*, 6) These are not demonstrable moral principles of natural law but "mere artificial contrivances for the convenience and advantage of society." (*Ibid.*, 5)

3 / Other Examples

Even though J. S. Mill is essentially a cognitivist (see Chap. 4, III, 2), his metaethical views are often similar

* We can see now that Hart's use of the term 'natural law' is similar to that of Hobbes, and especially of Hume. However, unlike Hume, Hart considers those ends which men in fact pursue to be *proper* ends, and demonstrably so.

to those of Hume. The mere fact that we "believe that we have natural feelings for justice" is no ground

to acknowledge them as an ultimate criterion of conduct. . . . Mankind are always predisposed to believe that any subjective feeling, not otherwise accounted for, is a revelation of some objective reality. (*Utilitarianism*, v)

Moral principles cannot be justified on the basis of intuition. Nor can they be demonstrated by deductive reasoning. "Questions of ultimate ends are not amenable to direct proof. Whatever can be proven to be good, must be so by being shown to be a means to something admitted to be good without proof." (*Utilitarianism*, i)* Only instrumental value judgments can be "proved" or, rather, empirically verified.

These criticisms of intuitionism are, of course, quite compatible with the naturalistic metaethics of *Utilitarianism*. However, in the last chapter of *A System of Logic*, Mill argues even against the naturalistic form of cognitivism and comes at least close to taking the noncognitivist position. He points out that "practical ethics, or morality," is customarily included under the term moral science but "improperly" so, since moral principles are expressed not in the indicative mood as are the sciences but in the imperative mood "or in periphrases equivalent to it."

Now, the imperative mood is the characteristic of art, as distinguished from science. Whatever speaks in rules or precepts, not in assertions respecting matters of fact, is art; and ethics, or morality, is properly a portion of the art corresponding to the sciences of human nature and society. The method, therefore, of ethics can be no other than that of art, or practice, in general. (VI, xii, 1)

---

* Similarly, Bentham's rhetorical question: Is the principle of utility "susceptible of any direct proof? It should seem not; for that which is used to prove everything else, cannot itself be proved." (*Principles*, i)

Yet it is precisely the method of *science* which Mill uses in *Utilitarianism* to justify the moral principle of utility. That the general happiness is intrinsically desirable is based on the "fact" that everyone desires his own happiness (and on the definition of 'desirable'). In *A System of Logic*, the role of science is reduced to the determination of the means, while "the definition of the end itself belongs exclusively to art and forms its peculiar province." (*Ibid.*, 5) The only fact referred to by intrinsic moral judgments is "that the conduct recommended excites in the speaker's mind the feeling of approbation." (*Ibid.*) Now there must be "some one principle, some rule or standard with which all other rules of conduct [are] required to be consistent"; otherwise "the same conduct might be approved by one of those principles and condemned by another, and there would be needed some more general principle as umpire between them." (*Ibid.*, 6) We have seen (Chap. 2, I, 3, a) that the adoption of *some* consistent set of normative principles is a requirement of rationality and, as such, is compatible with noncognitivism as well as with cognitivism.*

But Mill's readers are bound to ask: Is there a "method of art" by which overall standards of morality can be objectively determined? After having excluded intuition, deduction, and induction, what method could there be? Mill does not propose to give an answer "at this place," but merely declares his "conviction" that "the happiness of mankind" is "the general principle to which all rules of practice ought to conform." And then there is this footnote: "For an express discussion and *vindication* of this principle, see the little volume entitled 'Utilitarianism'." (*Ibid.*, 7; italics added) And so, after having been led to the threshold of non-

---

* The requirement of consistency does not imply, however, that there be "some *one* principle" from which all other rules of conduct can be deduced.

cognitivism, we are invited to return to the method of science for the foundation of morality.

Contemporary noncognitivism has been influenced not only by Humean empiricism but also by modern logical analysis and linguistic philosophy, itself an outgrowth of empiricism. This development has led to the distinction (not made by Hobbes and Hume) between that particular form of *subjectivism* which holds that '*x* is good' *means* that the speaker approves of *x*, and *emotivism*, according to which such utterances have no cognitive meaning but *express* the speaker's approval of *x*. We have seen that noncognitivism has adopted this latter view, thereby adding a criticism of the definist theory to Hume's arguments against intuitionism and the simpler form of naturalism. Indeed, if valuational and ethical terms have no cognitive meaning but only an expressive and directive function, then intrinsic valuational and ethical judgments cannot be cognitively either true or false.

Marxism is another movement which has influenced contemporary noncognitivism, especially in its application to social and political ethics. However, Marx himself did not deal explicitly with metaethical problems. Like Hume, he approached ethics as a subject matter of descriptive science. He aimed at explaining why particular groups hold particular moral views at particular times. His answer was that ethical norms, and especially principles of social and political ethics, are adopted as—often unconscious—rationalizations of economic interests by the dominant class at every stage of the ongoing class struggle. Addressed to the contemporary bourgeoisie, the *Communist Manifesto* declares:

The selfish misconception that induces you to transform into eternal laws of nature and reason the social forms springing from your present mode of production . . . you share with every ruling class that has preceded you.

Every ruling class claims objective validity for its professed moral principles; but this philosophy is always a misconception as well as a hypocritical concealment of material interests. The suppressed class tends to be well aware of such ideological disguises. This is true, e.g., of the nineteenth-century proletarian. "Law, morality, religion are to him so many bourgeois prejudices, behind which lurk in ambush just as many bourgeois interests." (*Ibid.*)

However, the empirical theory of cultural relativism cannot be used as an argument against value-cognitivism. A cognitivist may realize that different economic classes and social groups tend to adopt different, and often conflicting, moral and political doctrines, and yet he may hold that some of them are demonstrably true and others demonstrably mistaken. Similarly, a certain moral principle cannot be invalidated by pointing out that it functions as an ideological disguise of certain material interests. Both the ethical theory that all men should have certain legal rights and the metaethical theory that these rights are "natural" were adopted by members of the upcoming commercial middle class because it served their particular economic and political interests. This fact does not refute the cognitivist's claim that the moral principle: 'these legal rights ought to be protected' is demonstrably true. If this particular theory of natural law, or value-cognitivism in general, is mistaken, it must be on grounds such as those adduced by Hume. Even so, once political thinkers became aware of the ideological connection between political doctrines and political interests, they were bound to become more skeptical as to the claim that such principles are manifestations of objective and eternal truths.

Just as the diversity of ethical valuations is no valid argument in favor of noncognitivism, so cognitivism cannot be supported by the fact that certain ethical convictions are widely accepted by different classes and groups and within different cultures. This point was made by Max Weber, perhaps the most outspoken noncognitivist among social scientists before the first World War. (See Weber, p. 13) Weber assigned to the empirical social sciences the strictly limited, but nevertheless important, task of answering such questions as: Is the contemplated goal attainable at all? Is it compatible with other goals? What are the means necessary to bring it about? What would be the further consequences? (pp. 18, 20–21) These are precisely the conditions of rationality. (See Chap. 2, I, 3) When it comes to the question whether or not the state of affairs which includes the contemplated goal *should* be brought about, we are confronted with "irreducible evaluations" (p. 20), with "the making of a decision," and this "is not a task which science can undertake; it is rather the task of the acting, willing person. . . . The act of choice itself is his own responsibility." (p. 53) "It involves will and conscience, not empirical knowledge." (p. 54)

Even such simple questions as the extent to which an end should sanction unavoidable means, or the extent to which undesired repercussions should be taken into consideration, or how conflicts between several concretely conflicting ends are to be arbitrated, are entirely matters of choice and compromise. There is no (rational or empirical) scientific procedure of any kind whatsoever which can provide us with a decision here. The social sciences, which are strictly empirical sciences, are the least fitted to presume to save the individual the difficulty of making a choice, and they should therefore not create the impression that they can do so. (pp. 18–19)

Anticipating such modern noncognitivists as Stevenson and Hare, Weber holds that "the 'value-judgment' involves my 'taking an attitude' in a certain concrete way to the object in its concrete individuality." (p. 150) Hence,

it is simply naïve to believe . . . that it is possible to establish and to demonstrate as scientifically valid "a principle" for practical social science from which the norms for the solution of practical problems can be unambiguously derived. (p. 56)

Max Weber's conclusion that nothing can relieve man of his responsibility for making his own choices has been the central theme of existentialism. The revival of this philosophy in Continental Europe parallels the development of Anglo-American linguistic philosophy. Both movements are essentially noncognitivist, even though there has been little cross-fertilization between them. Let us take as an example perhaps the most influential recent existentialist work, Jean-Paul Sartre's *Existentialism Is a Humanism.** Since "God does not exist,"

there disappears with Him all possibility of finding values in an intelligible heaven. There can no longer be any good *a priori*, since there is no infinite and perfect consciousness to think it. It is nowhere written that "the good" exists, that one must be honest or must not lie, since we are now upon the plane where there are only men. (p. 33)

Even though atheists may be value-cognitivists, Sartre does not, at least in this passage, find it necessary to argue against naturalism or intuitionism based on moral or rational insight. In any case, Sartre concludes that man creates his own values. "If I regard a certain course of action as good, it is only I who choose to say that it is good and not bad." (p. 31) Someone else may choose to disapprove of the same action, and to act accordingly.

Thus we have neither behind us, nor before us in a luminous realm of values, any means of justification or excuse. We are left alone, without excuse. That is what I mean when I say that man is condemned to be free. (p. 34)

Man cannot escape the freedom, the necessity, and the responsibility of making his own decisions. "He is re-

* Even though Sartre himself has since repudiated many of the thoughts contained in this lecture.

sponsible for everything he does." (p. 34) This is meant to be a purely factual statement. My choices are not determined or even influenced either by God or by circumstances or by other men. Even if someone else "compels" me to act in a certain way, I am still free to disregard the threat. This is, of course, perfectly compatible with the view that all events, including my actual choices and actions, are in principle causally determined. Yet Sartre maintains that "there is no determinism—man is free, man *is* freedom." (p. 34) This is not to say that it does not matter how we choose. On the contrary, there is a strong normative dimension in Sartre's philosophy. We ought not to shirk our responsibilities. We ought to have the courage of our convictions, regardless of merely utilitarian considerations. Our choices should be based on serious, reflective, and authentic commitments. "In the end, it is feeling that counts; the direction in which it is really pushing me is the one I ought to choose." (p. 36) In what direction my feeling ought to push me is left undetermined. Like noncognitivism in general, existentialism is logically compatible with any substantive theory of private or public morality. Sartre himself became a Marxist while Heidegger, another existentialist, capitulated to National Socialism.

Contemporary philosophers, and political scientists as well, remain sharply divided on the central issue of moral philosophy. However, noncognitivism is the assumption underlying most modern writings dealing with empirical political research. It is also the dominant view among political theorists at the present time. One example, which is representative of the prevailing view, may suffice.

Facts and values are logically heterogeneous. The factual aspect of a proposition refers to a part of reality; hence it can be tested by reference to the facts. In this way we check its truth. The moral aspect of a proposition, however, expresses only the emotional response of an individual to a state of real or presumed facts. It indicates whether and the extent to which an individual desires a particular state of affairs to exist. Although we can say that the aspect of a proposition referring to a fact can be true or false, it is meaningless to characterize the value aspect of a proposition this way. (Easton, p. 221)

It seems to me that noncognitivism has refuted each of the claims advanced by the various cognitivist schools. Although I have dealt explicitly with only a small number of cognitivist theories, I believe that these are representative examples, and that others could easily fit into one or another of our categories. Some radically different cognitivist theory might be developed in the future, but I doubt such a possibility. This is not to say that I consider the whole debate closed. A number of finer points remain controversial; these are, however, at best only of marginal interest for political philosophy. With these qualifications, I conclude that none of the cognitivist arguments seems to stand up under the noncognitivist thrust, and the metaethics of cognitivism in any of its varieties becomes then untenable. If cognitivism in general is false, then its denial, noncognitivism, must be true. This reason is surely not the only basis for my conviction that noncognitivism is the correct metaethical theory. I believe also that its analysis of the logic of moral discourse is on the right track—a further reason for the probable failure of any future attempt at finding objective grounds for intrinsic moral principles.

Moral utterances guide conduct and alter behavior, but naturalism and intuitionism in effect treat moral utterances as property-ascribing theoretical utterances. To regard moral utterances in such a way is to miss their distinctive function. In using moral language, we do not, at least typically, tell someone *that* something is the case; we tell someone *to make* something the case . . . Fundamental moral claims are not matters of knowledge but expressions of attitude, decisions of principle, or declarations of intention. (Nielsen, p. 129)

II *Rebuttal of Cognitivist Counterattacks*

Cognitivists have taken the counteroffensive by claiming that noncognitivism entails certain views which its proponents would want to disclaim. How noncognitivists refute these arguments concerns us next.

1 / Noncognitivism and Irrationalism

Noncognitivism has been held to be incompatible with rationalism and therefore to entail irrationalism. The epistemological theory of rationalism affirms that substantive knowledge can be gained without reference to sense experience, e.g., by pure reasoning. Value-cognitivists of the intuitionist variety are rationalists, since they base valuational and moral principles on reason or insight.* Since noncognitivism denies the possibility of intrinsic valuational knowledge, it is for this reason alone incompatible with rationalism at least in matters of valuation. But value-cognitivists of the naturalistic school are not rationalists either, since they deny that values can be known by *a priori* methods. Hence, if noncognitivists could justifiably be labeled irrationalists, so could naturalists. Actually, this term should not be applied to either. The opposite of rationalism is empiricism, not irrationalism. Empiricism is the epistemological theory that all knowledge that is not purely analytic rests on sense experience. Rationalism and empiricism are not concerned with the possible extent of knowledge but with the method by which it can be gained or the grounds on which it can be justified. In-

---

* Rationalism is often defined more narrowly as the claim that reason is the only source of knowledge, to the exclusion of faith and intuition. In this sense, Grotius is a rationalist but Augustine is not. For various other meanings of this term, see Oppenheim, 1964, *passim*.

tuitionists are rationalists; naturalists are empiricists; value-noncognitivists are neither, as they do not consider values to be a matter of knowledge. They are not irrationalists, however.

Many of the thinkers we have examined hold one epistemological theory with respect to facts and another with respect to values. It is true that naturalists are necessarily empiricists with respect to both, since they regard ethics itself as an empirical science (e.g., Bentham). While value-noncognitivists tend to be empiricists when it comes to factual knowledge (e.g., Hume), other noncognitivists as to values may be rationalists as to facts (e.g., Hobbes). Intuitionists, who are rationalists as far as values are concerned (e.g., Plato or Locke), may or may not be rationalists with respect to the knowledge of facts (Plato was, but Locke was an empiricist).

The term rationalism has also been used in reference to the theory that there are objective criteria of rational choice. Taken in this sense, the opposite of rationalism *is* irrationalism, i.e., the denial of the possibility of ascertaining whether a choice is rational. We have seen that noncognitivists as well as cognitivists affirm that there are criteria of rational choice with respect to a given standard of evaluation, and that it is often possible to give "good reasons" for our more particular moral principles. However, noncognitivists cannot provide any guidance to ultimate standards. Hence, it is argued, they are irrationalists as far as this most important question is concerned. If intrinsic value judgments are but expressions of subjective tastes, feelings, and preferences, then the most crucial and consequential moral decisions can only be arbitrary, capricious, and irrational. And since all further decisions down the means-end chain depend on the choice of the ultimate end, all of them become arbitrary also, however rational they may be in terms of the final goal. Thus, according to Leo Strauss, the rejection of natural right and of value-cognitivism in general "is bound to lead to disastrous consequences."

Our social science may make us very wise or clever as regards the means for any objectives we might choose. It admits being unable to help us in discriminating between legitimate and illegitimate, between just and unjust, objectives . . . . According to our social science, we can be or become wise in all matters of secondary importance, but we have to be resigned to utter ignorance in the most important respect: we cannot have any knowledge regarding the ultimate principles of our choices, i.e., regarding their soundness or unsoundness; our ultimate principles have no other support than our arbitrary and hence blind preferences. (1953, pp. 3–4)

Similarly, John Wild criticizes the "extreme irrationalism" of the "noncognitive or emotive theory of ethics which reduces the whole phenomenon of obligation to the subjective compulsion of raw appetite or desire." (Wild, p. 215).

Even if the charge of irrationalism were warranted, it would apply to a small number of choices only, especially in the area of politics. Ultimate political goals are most often stated in terms which are so general that hardly anyone—at least among those who are on speaking terms—would deny being committed to them. Who wouldn't want government to pursue "the general welfare," "equality of opportunity," or "the national interest"? Two contemporary thinkers as different as J. S. Mill and Karl Marx shared the same ultimate goal of a society "in which the free development of each would be the condition of the free development of all." (*Communist Manifesto*) The great majority of political disagreements are not about the "grand alternatives" * but about the implementation of commonly

---

* This expression is borrowed from Dahl and Lindblom, page 3. Verbal agreement about such grand alternatives may, of course,

agreed ends, and these questions do fall within the scope of rationality.

Still, there are those important disagreements about "ultimate principles" such as the intrinsic desirability of racial discrimination, birth control, death penalty, conscientious objection. I believe that noncognitivism need not deny the applicability of rationality even in this area. The contrary view is based on an oversimplified conception of the decision-making process. Actors in general and political actors and theorists in particular do not normally first pick out some "ultimate goal" such as "curbing Communist aggression anywhere" and then let social science determine the most effective means, in this instance possibly the use of nuclear weapons. To act rationally, it is not sufficient to predict a chain of events leading from the contemplated immediate action via intermediate goals to the ultimate end. The picture of a network would be more appropriate. A rational actor must predict, as best he can, the *total* outcome of his contemplated course of action, which includes not only the "means" and the "ultimate end" but also side effects and ulterior consequences. He must consider every alternative course of action open to him in the given situation and predict the total outcome of each of these alternatives. This will enable him to determine whether his contemplated goal is compatible with other ends to which he has already committed himself.

Criteria of rationality apply not only to predictions but also to evaluations. To be rational, the actor's evaluations must reflect his actual preferences. To that effect, he must evaluate not some isolated goal but the total predicted outcome, taking into account elements which he would disvalue if he considered them in isolation. It may turn out that the negative utility of some

be deceptive; different political actors and thinkers may assign quite different meanings to the terms in which these goals are stated.

"means" or "side effect" outweighs the positive utility of the original, but tentative, "ultimate goal." Hence, the latter will not be included in the outcome which turns out to be the preferred alternative.

Political actors and thinkers sometimes single out one goal as so valuable that it outweighs whatever negative utility other aspects of the outcome might have. For instance, Hobbes considered peace and security such a goal, worth purchasing even at the price of tyranny. He realized that "the condition of subjects is very miserable; as being obnoxious to the lusts, and other irregular passions of him, or them that have so unlimited a power in their hands." (*Leviathan*, xviii) However, he regarded this outcome as a lesser evil than the only alternative—civil war. (*Ibid.*) But the majority of political theories are pluralistic rather than monistic; i.e., they consider more than one state of affairs to be intrinsically desirable; they tend to recommend not pursuing a single goal at any price but drawing a balance between competing goals such as individual freedom and economic security, rewards according to ability and according to need, peace—but not at any price.

The question how much of one goal must be sacrificed in order to come to a closer approximation (by how much?) of a competing goal can in principle be answered rationally, and hence objectively. *How* to draw the balance is, according to noncognitivism, the only question which is a matter of subjective preference, not objective rationality. Subjective preferences are, then, in general expressed as rank-orderings of alternative possible total outcomes. Relative to the actor's overall state of preferences (and relative to his state of information), the criteria of rationality are applicable. Given an actor's overall pattern of preferences, his choice of a course of action is rational if, and only if, its expectable total outcome is more valuable to him than (or rather, at least as valuable to him as) the total outcome of each alternative. This relative concept of rationality is defined in terms of an objective standard. For example, did the actor, in his evaluation of some predicted possible outcome, take into consideration all its significant aspects? Did he evaluate each alternative outcome correctly in terms of his overall preferences? That there are intrinsic valuational and moral issues which cannot be settled by rational argument does not entail that "our ultimate principles have no other support than our arbitrary and hence blind preferences." Commitment to a moral principle, and especially to a principle of political ethics, brings with it the implicit endorsement of a whole network of consequences. While such a commitment cannot be shown to be in itself legitimate or illegitimate, right or wrong, rational or irrational, it can have the support of preferences which, relative to this commitment, are rational.

The cognitivist might, however, have a further objection: I do not deny that, as a matter of fact, you and most other noncognitivists have confidence in the empirical method and believe in the possibility of rational choice. But your position is inconsistent. If you are a value-noncognitivist, you must be a noncognitivist all around, and then you are an irrationalist in yet another sense of this term. You must deny that there are valid grounds for generalizations of any kind, be they valuational or factual or even purely formal. If you consider intrinsic value judgments to be a matter of subjective preference, you cannot claim objective validity for the "scientific method" and its results.

To this the noncognitivist would reply: I deny that basic moral principles are statement-making utterances at all, and this is the reason why I deny that they have cognitive status. If they lack cognitive status, the question how they can be proven or verified or otherwise validated cannot even arise. But this consideration has no bearing at all on the question whether and why we are justified in regarding genuine statements to be objectively true or false, be they factual or formal, particular or general. Noncognitivism as to values does not entail noncognitivism as to facts.

2 / Noncognitivism and Relativism

Noncognitivism has been criticized for being in some way linked to relativism—a word which, like irrationalism, has various meanings, each with negative connotations.

Relativism may be taken in the sense of cultural relativism, a theory of anthropology or sociology. This descriptive theory emphasizes, first of all, that ethical and political convictions may vary, not only from person to person but also from group to group, and that the moral code of any group is "relative to," and causally dependent on, its social and cultural environment. Hardly anyone would deny that ethical commitments vary in time and space, and that these variations can often be explained in terms of cultural factors. Cultural relativism makes the stronger claim that at least some of these differences concern *basic* moral principles and would therefore subsist even if all the relevant factual disagreements could be resolved. Cultural universalism, on the other hand, holds that there are certain moral principles which are accepted in all cultures or would be universally adopted if it were not for varieties of factual interpretations. Whether cultural relativism or cultural universalism is correct does not directly concern our topic. Both may be true with respect to different ethical principles. If there were universal agreement that there is no life after death, there would be universal condemnation of burning heretics to save their souls. On the other hand, we have seen that, even within our own society, people may agree on all the facts pertaining to birth control, the death penalty, or civil disobedience and yet continue to have opposite moral convictions about such issues.

If cultural relativism is true, even in a limited way

the question arises whether this descriptive theory supports the metaethical theory of noncognitivism. One often hears the argument: Look at the many diametrically opposed basic principles of morality which have been adopted in various societies concerning sexual relations, the killing of infants and the aged, political obligation and private property. The sciences of anthropology, sociology, economics, and politics are able to account for most of these differences. How can you, in the light of all evidence, still maintain that there is a single, universally valid moral code, and that all deviations are not only immoral but even erroneous? That this argument is fallacious was pointed out when we discussed the Marxist view that there is no "true" morality *because* the dominant moral principles in every society are "but" the product of the stage of its economic development. Different cultures have also adopted, at different times, different theories about the solar system, the causes of mental illness, the origin of the State, or the nature of sovereignty. These differences, too, can in most cases be accounted for by reference to sociological or even economic factors. Even so, nobody denies that of any two conflicting descriptive theories only one can be true. A cognitivist could argue that the varieties of ethical valuations merely indicate that some persons and groups adopt the "wrong" values. It would, of course, be just as mistaken to claim that some moral principle is correct because it is in fact adopted everywhere (as, e.g., Hart tends to argue, but not Hume). Noncognitivism, which I consider the correct metaethical theory, should not be supported by the incorrect argument from cultural relativism.

Obviously, the metaethical theories of both cognitivism and noncognitivism are compatible with the descriptive theories of both cultural relativism and cultural universalism. In fact, noncognitivists such as Hume have stressed the similarities among men's ultimate goals. On the other hand, a cognitivist such as

Aquinas was well aware of existing social and cultural variations. That is why he taught that the principles of natural law must be transformed by way of "particular determinations" into "human law" which differs from one society to another in certain respects.

Relativism may also designate a theory of normative ethics, namely, that everyone has the moral duty to conform to the moral and political principles which happen to be prevalent in his society. It may, accordingly, be morally right to practice polygamy, infanticide, slavery, or witch-burning in one social system and wrong in another. Noncognitivism does not entail normative ethical relativism. A noncognitivist may be a nonconformist. He may be committed to the role of conscientious objector even though the overwhelming majority in his society considers it morally wrong to refuse to bear arms. Conversely, a cognitivist may adhere to the moral principle that everyone ought to comply with the existing moral code and positive law whether or not he approves of it. The Socrates of Plato's *Crito* exemplifies this view.

Relativism refers not only to a descriptive or to an ethical theory but to a metaethical theory as well. Metaethical relativism holds that ethical *truth* is "relative"—relative to social conditions and cultural features. Under this assumption, there are at least some conflicting basic moral principles which are "equally true," that is, one of them is true in one society but not in another, and vice versa. Political theorists have sometimes argued that metaethical relativism is entailed by noncognitivism. Noncognitivism holds

that there is no rational assurance that disagreement about political principles and ideals can be resolved. This in turn implies that there is no justification for the common assumption that the incompatible views of totalitarian and democratic communities about the rights of the individual cannot both be true. (Murray, p. 224)

Similarly, it has been held that to claim

that normative theories have no scientific status whatever and are purely hortatory . . . is to maintain that Hitler's ideal for the state has exactly as good a cognitive (*sic!*) and moral status as Locke's or Jefferson's or Ghandi's. (Northrop, p. 282)

Noncognitivism does not entail metaethical relativism. Noncognitivism claims that *neither* of *any* two conflicting basic moral or political principles is *either* true or false. The relativist thesis that there are conflicting principles *both* of which *are* true presupposes, on the contrary, a cognitivist metaethics, namely, the definist theory that the expression: 'it is morally right for A to do *x*' means the same as: 'doing *x* is generally approved in A's society'. Then, if slavery is condoned in society A and condemned by society B, it follows indeed not only that practicing slavery is morally right in A and wrong in B but also that the statements: 'practicing slavery is right in A' and 'practicing slavery is wrong in B' are both true. Some anthropologists have taken this position. Ruth Benedict pleads for "a more realistic social faith" based on the "coexisting and equally valid patterns of life which mankind has created for itself from the raw materials of existence." (p. 278) Similarly, "the relativist point of view brings into relief the *validity* of every set of norms *for* the people whose lives are guided by them." (Herskovits, p. 76; quoted by Brandt, 1959, p. 288) Would these authors draw the logical conclusion that the set of norms which guided the lives of most Germans under Hitler was "valid" for Germany? This form of naturalism does entail both ethical and metaethical relativism. Noncognitivism, while compatible with the former, must deny the latter.*

---

* If, on the other hand, 'good' is taken as a synonym of 'conducive to happiness', then it is in principle possible to determine whether the outcome of any action or policy anywhere is intrinsically desirable. Some forms of naturalism are therefore incompatible with metaethical relativism, and so are all forms of intuitionism. Two conflicting moral principles cannot both be

Relativism is sometimes taken to refer to a different metaethical theory, namely, that there are at least some sets of two conflicting basic moral principles neither of which can be shown to be either true or false (see Beardsley and Beardsley, p. 537). Noncognitivists are of course relativists in this sense, since they hold that no ethical principle is either true or false. The same meta-ethical theory is sometimes invoked by cognitivists who argue that, if there is no method by which one can decide that one of two conflicting moral principles is more justified than the other, then they are both equally justified. I would take the noncognitivist position, not that both principles are true, but that neither can be considered either true or false.*

3 / Noncognitivism and Nihilism

Noncognitivists are most often accused of considering value words and value judgments to be devoid of meaning. Critics are saying that noncognitivists cannot therefore logically make value statements at all. "If there is no sacred, eternal, divine, absolute law, there is no possibility of denouncing any form of law or policy or national act as unjust." (Brunner, p. 8) Accordingly, noncognitivism is held to entail "the prohibition against value judgments in social science." (Strauss, 1953, p. 52) The "ethical positivist," i.e., the noncognitivist

does not say, "There is an objective 'good' but we cannot prove what it is." What he does say is that the statement

---

"self-evident" or in conformity with moral insight or revelation (but the injunction that everyone ought to conform to the prevailing moral code of his society can).

* Political theorists sometimes use 'relativism' as a synonym of 'noncognitivism'. Arnold Brecht speaks of "Scientific Value Relativism" in this sense (Brecht, p. 117). Hans Kelsen speaks of "philosophical relativism which recognizes only relative truth and relative values" (Kelsen, p. 199); this may refer to ethical or metaethical or even to cultural relativism.

"Democracy is good" is meaningless because the whole question at issue is meaningless. (Pennock, p. 53, fn. 33)

If so, "everything a man is willing to dare will be permissible. The contemporary rejection of natural right leads to nihilism—nay, it is identical with nihilism." (Strauss, 1953, pp. 4–5) Noncognitivism and secularism represent

a form of scepticism which is conscious of the relativity of all human perspectives. In this form it stands on the abyss of moral nihilism and threatens the whole of life with a sense of meaninglessness. (Niebuhr, 1944, p. 133)

And so it is asked: "For how can you condemn a tyrant as unjust when you have purged the word justice from your vocabulary?" (Hallowell, p. 326). I think I can. I have not excluded the word 'justice' from my vocabulary. I do not claim that the statement: 'democracy is good' is meaningless. I do not prohibit social scientists and others from making value judgments. I do maintain that value words, and intrinsic value judgments in which they occur, have expressive and directive, rather than cognitive, meanings. I do deny the possibility of *demonstrating* that democracy is good and tyranny evil (except in relation to a set of given goals or standards or valuations). This need not, and does not, prevent me from expressing my approval of democracy and denouncing tyranny. It is one thing to commit oneself to some moral principle; it is another to claim that it is demonstrable. Noncognitivism does not entail nihilism.

The same criticism, when applied to the legal sphere, leads to the view that the denial of natural law entails legal positivism, in the sense that 'just' is synonymous with: 'commanded or permitted by some positive legal rule'. "To reject natural right is tantamount to saying that all right is positive right, and this means that what is right is determined exclusively by the legislators and the courts of various countries." (Strauss, 1953, p. 2) However, that all law is positive law and all right positive right means that what is *legal*, not what is *moral*, is determined by legislators and courts. It is true that certain noncognitivists, e.g., Hobbes, do hold that the concepts of just and unjust are meaningless except in a legal sense. But noncognitivism by no means necessarily entails legal positivism in this sense, as is claimed by a recent decision of the German Federal Supreme Court: "The idea that the original constituent power may ordain anything according to mere will would be a relapse into the spirit of value-free legal positivism." (Cited by Rommen, pp. 19–20) Of course, it may do so; but to acknowledge this possibility is not to deny that "experience under the Nazi regime has taught that even the legislator may posit injustice." (*Ibid.*) Noncognitivists can, with perfect consistency, maintain that an action, though legally right, is morally wrong, or that a law, though legally valid (e.g., constitutional), is unjust from a moral point of view. They merely deny that it is possible to give objective grounds for moral judgments about positive law (except, again, in terms of some previously adopted values).

Noncognitivists do tend toward legal positivism in a different sense, namely, that "the existence of law is one thing; its merit or demerit is another" (Austin, *Jurisprudence*, Lecture V; see above Chap. 2, II, 1, b), and that a legal enactment remains a law even when it is deemed unjust. Cognitivists, and especially proponents of the natural law thesis, often define the concept of law persuasively to designate those, and only those, legal rules which they claim to be demonstrably just and in conformity with natural law. Nevertheless, legal positivism in the sense of the separation between law and morality is compatible with cognitivism as well as with noncognitivism.

Legal positivism (in the sense of: what is legal is right) is held to lead in turn to the ethical view that might makes right, and hence to the active support, or at least the passive acceptance, of totalitarian might.

Of the many factors which have contributed to the decline of liberalism in the modern world no single factor has been more important than the rise of positivism and its infiltration into every sphere of thought. For it was the liberal, positivistic jurists long before Hitler who taught (explicitly or implicitly) that might makes right and that rights are not attributes which individuals have by virtue of their humanity but simply claims which the state may or may not choose to recognize. Unwittingly, it may be, such liberals prepared the way for Lidice and Dachau. (Hallowell, p. 326)

The totalitarian state is simply and solely legal positivism in political practice, the abrogation in actual fact of the classical and Christian idea of a divine "law of nature." (Brunner, p. 7)

Contrariwise, commitment to democracy and liberty is viewed as presupposing the philosophy of cognitivism. "A dogmatic belief in objective value is necessary to the very idea of a rule which is not tyranny or an obedience which is not slavery." (Lewis, p. 46)

This claim and the previous one cannot both be warranted. If noncognitivism entails nihilism, i.e., moral indifference, noncognitivism cannot entail a specific system of political ethics, authoritarianism. Both accusations are equally unfounded. Noncognitivism implies neither that the choice between liberalism and authoritarianism is meaningless, nor that one is as good as the other, nor that the latter is desirable or tolerable. And the opposite view, that authoritarianism presupposes a cognitivist metaethics, is just as mistaken.* The reason is always the same: there is no logical connection between any theory about the possibility of valuational knowledge and any system of values; every metaethical philosophy is logically compatible with every theory of

* For example, Murray, p. 231; Kelsen, p. 204.

political ethics. All possible combinations are not only logically consistent but can also, as a matter of fact, be found among political thinkers, as we saw in connection with the natural law theory and its denial (Chap. 2, II, 2). For example, Plato considered absolute rule to be objectively the best form of government. On the other hand, Locke taught that a limited government confining itself to the protection of basic rights is in accordance with natural law. Among noncognitivists, Hobbes advocated an absolute form of government and Bertrand Russell is a proponent of liberal democracy.

As a last stand, cognitivists argue as follows: Granted that, logically, noncognitivism is compatible with rational behavior and with ethical commitment. However, from a psychological point of view,

once we realize that the principles of our actions have no other support than our blind choice, we really do not believe in them any more. We cannot *wholeheartedly* act upon them any more. We cannot live any more as *responsible* beings. . . . The inescapable *practical* consequence of nihilism is fanatical obscurantism. (Strauss, 1953, p. 6; italics added)

Except on the premises of this philosophy [of natural law], it is impossible to reach intelligible and *workable* conceptions of popular election, majority rule, representative assemblies, free speech, loyalty, property, corporations and voluntary associations. (Lippmann, pp. 79–80; italics added)

Serious and dedicated commitment to a system of political ethics is held to be impossible unless it is *demonstrably* desirable. "A dogmatic belief in objective value" in general, and in the objective value of democracy in particular, is deemed necessary to be a *convinced* democrat; without the foundation of cognitivism, liberty cannot be a *fighting* creed. On a more practical, legal level, natural law is viewed as a bulwark against the onslaughts of totalitarianism, while its denial makes it a least easier for dictators to translate their arbitrary will into positive law. Perhaps this is how some of the passages quoted in the previous section are to be interpreted.

Even if it were true that noncognitivists can at best have lukewarm value commitments, this would of course be no argument against the *validity* of the noncognitivist thesis. This is like criticizing atomic physics because it has led to atomic armament. Here Hume's dictum becomes relevant: "When any opinion leads us into absurdities, it is certainly false; but it is not certain an opinion is false because it is of dangerous consequence." (*Treatise*, II, Part IV) Moreover, even if it were conceded that noncognitivists are inclined toward ethical skepticism, cognitivism leads to dogmatism—a far more dangerous consequence. While they may endorse freedom of opinion, holders of political power who are convinced that they are in possession of moral truth are often psychologically inclined to suppress deviations from orthodoxy not only as erroneous but also as sinful. The natural law theory, in particular, is a two-edged sword. While the pompous self-righteousness of the postwar German courts at least points in the "right" direction, the Nazis—had *they* won the war—might well have claimed that their legislation is not contrary to but in accord with some objective "higher" law. Their argument would have been neither more nor less erroneous, since the natural law theory itself and value-cognitivism in general is mistaken. This points to a practical maxim: If you start a war, you had better win it, because natural law will go with the victor.

This is to say that democratic cognitivists, too, are capable of intolerance. We are told that communism is a heresy which cannot be defeated in the cold war of ideas without a counterreligion. This is one of the reasons why cognitivism remains popular in the United States, while noncognitivism is often considered not just mistaken, but subversive. And so our—official and

unofficial—spokesmen indulge in cognitivist language
with its moralizing and self-righteous overtones. We do
not merely praise our democratic way of life; we claim
that we can *prove* that it is intrinsically the best, not
only for ourselves but for all others. We talk as if we,
and only we, are endowed with the insight of Plato's
guardians, and as if we were indeed the guardians of
the whole "free" world, morally and militarily.

Here again, historical evidence is ready to illustrate
that it is psychologically possible for noncognitivists to
be unswervingly committed to their chosen values generally, and for noncognitivist liberals to be dedicated to
the values of individual freedom. While in England
and the United States this ideology has traditionally
been linked to the metaethics of natural rights, in Continental Europe the most ardent defenders of individual
liberty and dignity against absolute government have
come from the ranks of the liberal and later socialist
movements; and their philosophical background has
been essentially agnostic, empiricist, and noncognitivist.
Presumably, most of the Jacobins of 1791, the Liberals
of 1848, the Loyalists of 1936, and the *Maquisards* of
1944 were willing to risk their lives for the sake of liberty simply because they had committed themselves to
this ideal, individually and collectively.

It may at first be frustrating to realize that there can
be no objective foundation for our most basic moral
and political convictions. Yet, it seems to me to be the
mark of a mature person and of a mature civilization to
be able to stand on one's own feet without the crutches
of what I hope I have shown to be a mistaken philosophy. Noncognitivism helps us to adjust to the necessity
of "coexistence" in a world half of which is not to our
liking. It helps us to realize that it is not only impossible
but also presumptuous to attempt to shape the rest of
the world in our image. It helps us to uphold the values
of human dignity—fervently, but with humility.

List of Works Cited

1 Classical Works

Aquinas, St. Thomas (1225–1274), *S.T.*, I–II
Summa Theologica. First Part of the Second Part, Questions 90–96. In *Introduction to Saint Thomas Aquinas*. Edited with an Introduction by Anton C. Pegis. New York: The Modern Library, 1948. By permission of Random House and Burns & Oates Ltd.

Aristotle (384–322 B.C.), *Ethics*
The Nicomachean Ethics. Translated by H. Rackham. London: William Heinemann, Ltd., 1962.

Aristotle, *Politics*
The Politics of Aristotle. Translated with an Introduction, Notes, and Appendixes by Ernest Barker. New York and London: Oxford University Press, 1946.

Augustine, St. (354–430), *Contra Faustum*
In Henry Paolucci (ed.), *The Political Writings of St. Augustine*. Chicago: Henry Regnery Co., 1962. The quotation is on p. 172.

Augustine, St., *De Trinitate*
In Herbert A. Deane, *The Political and Social Ideas of
St. Augustine.* New York: Columbia University Press,
1963. The quotation is on p. 87.

Augustine, St., *Enarrationes in Psalmos*
In Paolucci, *op. cit.,* pp. 153–154.

Augustine, St., *In Iohannis Evangelium Tractatus*
In Deane, *op. cit.,* p. 285.

Austin, John (1790–1859), *Jurisprudence*
*The Province of Jurisprudence Determined and The
Uses of the Study of Jurisprudence.* With an Introduction by H. L. A. Hart. London: Weidenfeld and Nicol-
son, 1954. (The former work was first published in
1832.)

Bentham, Jeremy (1748–1832), *Principles*
*An Introduction to the Principles of Morals and Legisla-
tion.* (1789) Numerous editions.

Burke, Edmund (1729–1797), *Hastings*
Speech on the Impeachment of Warren Hastings. (1788)
Numerous editions.

Calvin, John (1509–1564), *Institutes*
Institutes of the Christian Religion. (First Latin edition,
1559) Edited by John T. McNeil. Translated by Ford
Lewis Battles. Philadelphia: Westminster Press, 1960.

Cicero, Marcus Tullius (106–43 B.C.), *Laws*
De Re Publica De Legibus. With an English Translation
by Clinton W. Keyes. London: William Heinemann,
Ltd., 1928.

Cicero, Marcus Tullius, *Republic*
Loc. cit.

Grotius, Hugo (1583–1645), *De Jure Belli ac Pacis*
De Jure Belli ac Pacis Libri Tres. (1625) Translated by
Francis W. Kelsey. Oxford: At the Clarendon Press,
1925.

Hobbes, Thomas (1588–1679), *De Cive*
De Cive or The Citizen. (1642) Edited with an Intro-
duction by Sterling P. Lamprecht. New York: Appleton-
Century-Crofts, Inc., 1949.

Hobbes, Thomas, *Elements of Law*

Elements of Law Natural and Politic. Edited by Ferdinand Tönnies. London, 1889. Quoted by Frederick A. Olafson, "Thomas Hobbes and the Modern Theory of Natural Law," *Journal of the History of Philosophy*, IV (January 1966), 15–30. At p. 20, fn. 6.

Hobbes, Thomas, *Leviathan*
(1651) Numerous editions.

Hume, David (1711–1776), *Essays*
Essays: Moral, Political, and Literary. (Vol. I, 1741; Vol. II, 1742) In *Hume's Moral and Political Philosophy.* Edited with an Introduction by Henry D. Aiken. New York: Hafner Publishing Co., 1948.

Hume, David, *Human Understanding*
An Enquiry Concerning Human Understanding. (1748) Numerous editions.

Hume, David, *Principles of Morals*
An Enquiry Concerning the Principles of Morals. (1751) In Aiken, *op. cit.*

Hume, David, *Treatise*
A Treatise of Human Nature. (Books I and II, 1739; Book III, 1740) In Aiken, *op. cit.*

Immortale Dei
Encyclical Immortale Dei. (Pope Leo XIII, 1885) In Gerard F. Yates, S.J. (ed.), *Papal Thoughts on the State.* New York: Appleton-Century-Crofts, Inc., 1958.

Kant, Immanuel (1724–1804), *Metaphysics of Morals*
Foundations of the Metaphysics of Morals (Grundlegung zur Metaphysik der Sitten). (1785) Translated with an Introduction by Lewis White Beck. New York: The Liberal Arts Press, 1959.

Locke, John (1632–1704), *An Essay Concerning Human Understanding*
(1690) Numerous editions.

Locke, John, *Civil Government*
An Essay Concerning the True Original, Extent and End of Civil Government. (1690) Numerous editions.

Machiavelli, Niccolò (1469–1527), *The Prince*
Il Principe. (First published, Rome, 1532) In *The Prince and The Discourses.* With an Introduction by

Max Lerner. New York: The Modern Library, 1950.

Marx, Karl (1818–1883), *Communist Manifesto*
Karl Marx and Friedrich Engels, *Manifesto of the Communist Party.* (1848) Numerous editions.

Mill, John Stuart (1806–1873), *On Liberty*
(1859) Numerous editions.

Mill, John Stuart, *A System of Logic*
(1843; 8th ed., London, 1872) In *John Stuart Mill's Philosophy of Scientific Method.* Edited with an Introduction by Ernest Nagel. New York: Hafner Publishing Co., 1950.

Mill, John Stuart, *Utilitarianism*
(1863) Numerous editions.

Montesquieu, Charles Louis de Secondat, Baron de (1689–1755), *Spirit of the Laws*
L'esprit des lois. (First published, 1748) Translated by Thomas Nugent. Two volumes. Cincinnati: Robert Clarke & Co., 1873.

Plato (427–347 B.C.), *Republic*
The Republic of Plato. Translated with an Introduction and Notes by Francis Macdonald Cornford. New York and London: Oxford University Press, 1941.

Rousseau, Jean-Jacques (1712–1778), *Discourse on Inequality*
Discours sur l'origine et les fondements de l'inégalité parmi les hommes. (First published, Amsterdam, 1755) In *The Social Contract and Discourses.* Translated with an Introduction by G. D. H. Cole. New York: E. P. Dutton and Company, Inc., 1950. (The quotation is on pp. 226–227.)

Rousseau, Jean-Jacques, *Emile*
(First published, 1762) Translated by Barbara Foxley. London: J. M. Dent and Sons, Ltd., 1911.

Rousseau, Jean-Jacques, *Letters from the Mountain*
Lettres écrites de la montagne. (First published, Amsterdam, 1764) In C. E. Vaughan (ed.), *The Political Writings of Jean-Jacques Rousseau.* Two volumes. New York: John Wiley & Sons, 1962. (The quotation is in Vol. II, p. 200. Translation mine.)

Rousseau, Jean-Jacques, *Political Economy*
Discours sur l'économie politique. (First published, Geneva, 1758) In Cole, *op. cit.* (The quotations are on pp. 289–291.)

Rousseau, Jean-Jacques, *Social Contract*
Du contrat social. (First published, Amsterdam, 1762) In Cole, *op. cit.*

Spencer, Herbert (1820–1903), *Data of Ethics*
(1879) New York: D. Appleton and Co., 1901.

Spencer, Herbert, *Essays*
"Progress: Its Law and Cause" (1857), in *Essays: Scientific, Political, and Speculative.* New York: D. Appleton and Co., 1907. Three volumes. (Vol. I, pp. 8–62)

Spencer, Herbert, *First Principles*
(1862) 4th American ed. New York: De Witt Revolving Fund, Inc., 1958.

Spencer, Herbert, *Social Statics*
(1855) 3rd American ed. New York: D. Appleton and Co., 1882.

Spencer, Herbert, *The Study of Sociology*
(1873) 9th ed. London: Williams and Norgate, 1880.

2   Works Published After 1900

Arendt, Hannah, "Truth and Politics." In David Spitz (ed.), *Political Theory of Social Change.* New York: Atherton Press, 1967, pp. 3–37.

Ayer, Alfred Jules, *Language, Truth and Logic.* 2d ed. New York: Dover Publications, Inc., 1946.

Baier, Kurt, *The Moral Point of View: A Rational Basis of Ethics.* Ithaca, N.Y.: Cornell University Press, 1958. By permission of Cornell University Press.

Beardsley, Monroe C., and **Elizabeth Lane Beardsley,** *Philosophical Thinking: An Introduction.* New York: Harcourt, Brace & World, Inc., 1965.

Benedict, Ruth, *Patterns of Culture.* Boston: Houghton Mifflin Co., 1934.

Benn, S. I., and **R. S. Peters,** *Social Principles and the*

Democratic State. London: George Allen & Unwin, Ltd., 1959.

Brandt, Richard B., *Ethical Theory.* Englewood Cliffs, N. J.: Prentice-Hall, Inc., 1959.

Brandt, Richard B., *Moral Philosophy and the Analysis of Language.* Lawrence, Kans.: Department of Philosophy, The University of Kansas Press, 1963.

Brecht, Arnold, *Political Theory: The Foundations of Twentieth-Century Political Thought.* Princeton, N. J.: Princeton University Press, 1959.

Brown, Brendan F., "The Natural Law, the Marriage Bond, and Divorce," *Fordham Law Review,* XXIV (1955), 83–102. Reprinted by permission of the *Fordham Law Review.*

Brunner, Emil, *Justice and the Social Order.* Translated by Mary Hottinger. New York: Harper and Brothers, 1945.

Carritt, E. F., *Ethical and Political Thinking.* Oxford: At the Clarendon Press, 1947.

Chroust, Anton-Hermann, "On the Nature of Natural Law." In Paul Sayre (ed.), *Interpretations of Modern Legal Philosophies.* New York: Oxford University Press, 1947, pp. 70–84.

Churchman, C. West, *Prediction and Optimal Decision: Philosophical Issues of a Science of Values.* Englewood Cliffs, N. J.: Prentice-Hall, Inc., 1961.

Cohen, Morris R., and Ernest Nagel, *An Introduction to Logic and Scientific Method.* New York: Harcourt, Brace & Co., 1934.

Copleston, Frederick C., *A History of Philosophy.* Vol. II. London: Burns Oates & Washbourne, 1959.

Dahl, Robert A., *Modern Political Analysis.* Englewood Cliffs, N. J.: Prentice-Hall, Inc., 1963.

Dahl, Robert A., and Charles E. Lindblom, *Politics, Economics, and Welfare.* New York: Harper and Brothers, 1953.

Easton, David, *The Political System: An Inquiry Into the State of Political Science.* New York: Alfred A. Knopf, Inc., 1953.

"Ethics," *The Catholic Encyclopedia.* New York: Robert Appleton Co. (15 vols.) Vol. V (1909), 556–565.

Frankena, William K., *Ethics.* Englewood Cliffs, N. J.: Prentice-Hall, Inc., 1963.

Frankena, William K., "Recent Conceptions of Morality." In Castaneda, Hector-Neri and George Nakhnikian (ed.), *Morality and the Language of Conduct.* Detroit: Wayne State University Press, 1965.

Friedrich, Carl Joachim, *Man and His Government.* New York: McGraw-Hill Book Co., Inc., 1963.

Hallowell, John H., *Main Currents in Modern Political Thought.* New York: Henry Holt and Company, 1950.

Hare, Richard M., *Freedom and Reason.* Oxford: At the Clarendon Press, 1963.

Hare, Richard M., *The Language of Morals.* Oxford: At the Clarendon Press, 1952.

Hart, H. L. A., *The Concept of Law.* Oxford: At the Clarendon Press, 1961. By permission of the Clarendon Press, Oxford.

Hempel, Carl G., *Fundamentals of Concept Formation in Empirical Science.* Chicago: The University of Chicago Press, 1952.

Hempel, Carl G., *Philosophy of Natural Science.* Englewood Cliffs, N. J.: Prentice-Hall, Inc., 1966.

Herskovits, Melville, *Man and His Works.* New York: Alfred A. Knopf, Inc., 1948.

Kelsen, Hans, *What Is Justice?* Berkeley and Los Angeles: University of California Press, 1960.

King, Martin Luther, *Why We Can't Wait.* New York: Harper & Row, Publishers, 1964.

Lenin, V. I., *The Tasks of the Youth Leagues.* An address delivered to the Third All-Russian Youth Communist League, October 2, 1920. Reprinted in *The Strategy and Tactics of World Communism,* Supplement I. Washington, D. C.: Government Printing Office, 1948.

Lewis, Clive S., *The Abolition of Man.* New York: The Macmillan Co., 1947.

Lippmann, Walter, *Essays in the Public Philosophy.* New York: Mentor Books, 1963.

Lipset, Seymour Martin, *Political Man: The Social Bases of Politics.* Garden City, N. Y.: Doubleday & Co., Inc., 1960.

Maritain, Jacques, *Man and the State.* Chicago: The University of Chicago Press, 1951.

Maritain, Jacques, *The Rights of Man and Natural Law.* London: Geoffrey Bles, 1958.

Moore, George Edward, *Principia Ethica.* Cambridge: At the University Press, 1903.

Morgenthau, Hans J., "The Mainsprings of American Foreign Policy: The National Interest vs. Moral Abstractions," *The American Political Science Review,* XLIV, No. 4 (December 1950), 833–854.

Murray, A. R. M., *An Introduction to Political Philosophy.* London: Cohen & West, 1953.

Niebuhr, Reinhold, *The Children of Light and The Children of Darkness.* New York: Charles Scribner's Sons, 1944.

Niebuhr, Reinhold, *An Interpretation of Christian Ethics.* New York: Harper & Brothers, 1935.

Nielsen, Kai, "Ethics, Problems of," *The Encyclopedia of Philosophy.* New York: The Macmillan Company and The Free Press; London: Collier-Macmillan, Ltd., 1967 (8 vols.) Vol. III, 117–134.

Northrop, F. S. C., *The Logic of the Sciences and the Humanities.* New York: The Macmillan Company, 1949.

Oppenheim, Felix E., *Dimensions of Freedom.* New York: St. Martin's Press and London: Macmillan & Co., Ltd., 1961.

Oppenheim, Felix E., "Rationalism and Liberalism," *World Politics,* XVI, No. 2 (January 1964), 341–361.

Pennock, J. Roland, *Liberal Democracy: Its Merits and Prospects.* New York: Rinehart and Company, Inc., 1950.

Rommen, Heinrich, "Natural Law in the Decisions of the Federal Supreme Court and of the Constitutional Courts in Germany," *Natural Law Forum,* IV (1959), 1–25.

Russell, Bertrand, *A History of Western Philosophy.* New York: Simon and Schuster, 1945.

Sartre, Jean-Paul, *Existentialism and Humanism*. Translated by Philip Mairet. London: Methuen and Co., Ltd., 1948.

Simpson, George Gaylord, *The Meaning of Evolution*. New York: New American Library, 1951. By permission of Yale University Press.

Stevenson, Charles L., *Ethics and Language*. New Haven: Yale University Press, 1944.

Strauss, Leo, *Natural Right and History*. Chicago: The University of Chicago Press, 1953.

Strauss, Leo, *What Is Political Philosophy? and Other Studies*. New York: The Free Press of Glencoe, 1959.

Taylor, Paul W., *The Moral Judgment: Readings in Contemporary Meta-Ethics*. Englewood Cliffs, N. J.: Prentice-Hall, Inc., 1963.

Weber, Max, *The Methodology of the Social Sciences*. Translated and Edited by Edward A. Shils and Henry A. Finch. New York: The Free Press of Glencoe, 1949.

Wild, John, *Plato's Modern Enemies and the Theory of Natural Law*. Chicago: The University of Chicago Press, 1953.

Index of Names

Index of Subjects